this
HEATED
place

Encounters in the
Promised Land

DEBORAH CAMPBELL

Douglas & McIntyre

VANCOUVER/TORONTO

Douglas & McIntyre
2323 Quebec Street, Suite 201
Vancouver, British Columbia
V5T 4S7
www.douglas-mcintyre.com

National Library of Canada Cataloguing in Publication Data
Campbell, Deborah, 1970–
   This heated place

   Includes bibliographical references
   ISBN 1-55054-967-7

   1. Campbell, Deborah, 1970– —Journeys—Palestine.
2. Palestine—Description and travel. 3. Palestine—Social conditions.
4. Arab-Israeli conflict. I. Title
DS107.5.C35 2002   915.69404'54   C2002-910861-6

Editing by Barbara Pulling
Copy-editing by Robin Van Heck
Cover photograph by Gary Braasch / Getty Images
Cover and text design by Val Speidel
Inside photographs by Deborah Campbell
Printed and bound in Canada by Friesens
Printed on acid-free paper

The publisher gratefully acknowledges the financial support of the Canada Council for the Arts, the British Columbia Ministry of Tourism, Small Business and Culture, and the Government of Canada through the Book Publishing Industry Development Program (BPIDP) for its publishing activities.

this **HEATED** place

Peace cannot be kept by force.
It can only be achieved by understanding.

—Albert Einstein

CONTENTS

PREFACE

I GREW UP ON STORIES OF the Promised Land. It was a mythical place, suspended halfway between heaven and earth, a haven for the exiled. As a girl attending church with my parents, I sat through long sermons grounded in this metaphorical terrain, which Christianity, originally a Jewish sect, had adopted as its own. Since exile is a state, at least a state of mind, that many of us experience at some point in our lives, the Promised Land holds universal appeal. It is a return to the "land of milk and honey." Is there a more poetic description of the mother's breast? But this Promised Land also has an earthly geography. It is the place, verifiable in an atlas, where the Jews in 1948 recreated their long-lost homeland.

The Promised Land—but promised to whom? Therein lies the world's longest-standing argument. In the Biblical account, God promised the land of Canaan—a region as vast as the Nile to the Euphrates—to Abraham and his offspring. But Abraham is the father of two nations—the Jews through Isaac (Abraham's son by his wife, Sarah) and the Arabs through Ishmael (Abraham's first-born son by Sarah's Egyptian servant, Hagar).

In the early years of high school, I became captivated by the story of the modern state of Israel. Had I been Jewish, I would have been an ardent

Zionist. I studied the Holocaust, a horror that both shocked and fasci-
nated in its magnitude, and gravitated to the novels of Leon Uris. In
Exodus, Uris wrote the definitive Western narrative of the creation of
modern-day Israel, reinforcing parallels between the Biblical journey out
of exile and the birth of the Zionist state. For Uris, the new Israelis were
bold, brave, moral; the Arabs vicious, cunning, cruel. His was the classic
tale of Israel, the fragile raft adrift on an ocean of hostile Arab states. It was
David versus Goliath, and it was impossible to side with any but handsome young David.

Following high school, I moved to Paris to study. A year later, obeying a fevered impulse, I enrolled at Tel Aviv University as a foreign student. In the summer of 1990, I arrived in Israel. Three days later, Iraq
invaded Kuwait.

That year, while studying Hebrew, Judaism, Islam, Zionism and the
politics and history of the Middle East, I learned to strap on a gas mask
and seal the doors of my campus apartment with packing tape, lest
Saddam do to us what he had done to the Kurds. The Israelis who
befriended me were kind and generous, in particular the family of a
physics professor who, without having met me, invited a student they
had heard was without family to stay in their home for the final weeks of
the Gulf War. At their kitchen table, I ate some of the best meals I had
that year and enjoyed some of the most enlightening conversation. To
them, I owe a debt of gratitude.

In many ways, it was in Israel that I began the necessary process of
distinguishing my views from those with which I had been raised.
Israelis seemed to thrive on debate; dissent was the whetstone on which
to hone their convictions. What impressed me most was their ability to
disagree vociferously, then fall back into closeness—to retain unity in
their diversity.

On returning to Canada to complete my university studies, I spent
time working for the Canadian Jewish Congress, a social justice organization whose Israeli director hired me because I spoke better Hebrew and

was better acquainted with Middle Eastern affairs than the Jewish applicants. It was fulfilling to be part of efforts to counter anti-Semitism and to meet Holocaust survivors who had overcome great trauma to share their stories. I remember being in the office on the day in 1995 when we learned that Israeli Prime Minister Yitzhak Rabin had been assassinated by a Jewish Israeli law student opposed to an Israeli withdrawal from the West Bank. I remember crying.

Yet, throughout those years, I do not remember hearing more than a cursory explanation of the Israeli occupation, nor any discussion of the reasons why Rabin had contemplated leaving lands conquered in 1967. Palestinians were almost invisible, a side story that distracted from the feature narrative of Zionism and the Jewish homeland. When the subject of the occupation *was* broached, it was usually to express the view that Palestinians should be grateful for the higher standard of living conferred upon them by Israel. ("Look at Egypt. Look at Jordan. Aren't the Palestinians better off?")

For all my so-called education, there was a knowledge gap. If it was to be filled, I would have to fill it myself.

In 2001, a decade after my first journey to Israel, I made up my mind to return. I wanted to explore how much had changed in the intervening years and to fill in the missing pieces, to ask the questions I had been unable to formulate in the past. I arrived to an escalating crisis. Two weeks after my arrival, the crisis was compounded by the attacks of September 11, events which fundamentally shifted regional politics in ways that continue to unfold.

"It's terrible to say, but the attacks are good for Israel," an Israeli from Tel Aviv told me. "Now America knows what the Arabs are like." His words echoed a sentiment that resounded through the Jewish population. Palestinians, on the other hand, greeted the attacks with trepidation. "You will tell them I was here. I didn't do it," said an Arab Israeli, joking darkly as we sat on his balcony in Haifa, gazing out at the Mediterranean on the evening of the fateful day. Israel's Prime Minister, Ariel Sharon, hastened to dub Yasser Arafat "our bin Laden" and linked the American "war on terror" with Israel's own war in the territories (which, freed momentarily from international pressures, was swiftly accelerated). Palestinians, by and large, preferred a conspiracy theory that charged the Israeli Mossad—or merely "the Jews"—with responsibility for the attacks.

In the three months I spent travelling in Israel, the West Bank and Gaza, I was mindful of the words of someone I met along the way. When it comes to understanding the myriad complexities of the Palestinian-Israeli conflict, he told me, "What you see depends on where you are standing." I essayed to emulate the approach of the journalist Martha Gellhorn, who wrote, of covering World War II, "I gave up trying to think or judge, and turned myself into a walking tape recorder with eyes." From the outset, I determined to present the facts as I found them, though without denying my own response. I did my best to resist the temptation, common to journalists in the region, to slice the conflict neatly down the middle and pass out half the blame to each side.

What follows is a personal account of my journey into twenty-first-century Israel and the occupied territories. It is not intended as a treatise, nor as a scoreboard of body counts and tit-for-tat atrocities. Rather, it is a look beyond the headlines into the lives of real people to better understand the conflict through their eyes. Some of these people have been given only a first name here, and in some cases that first name has been changed to respect the privacy, and the safety, of those who took me into their confidence.

My task was made easier by virtue of being neither Jewish nor Arab (nor Christian in more than upbringing) and—it would be naïve to overlook this—by virtue of being blue-eyed and blonde, characteristics that opened doors where journalistic credentials would not on their own have sufficed. Had I appeared Jewish or Arab, I would have faced obstacles that my obvious foreignness, and the neutrality it accorded, overcame. Had I been a man, I would surely have chosen other stories to tell.

There were several points at which I hesitated during the writing of this book. I know how heated this discussion can be, how it invokes the very emotions that fuel the engine of violence grinding its way through the Middle East. So I was encouraged to read the words of Edward Said, the renowned Palestinian scholar of Islam and the Arab world, who wrote, "Most knowledge about human society is, I think, finally accessible to common sense—that is, the sense that grows out of the common human experience." Most knowledge, and most solutions as well. It is the common human experience that I wish to convey.

I recently reread the final words from the speech Yitzhak Rabin gave the evening of his assassination to a peace rally in Tel Aviv attended by 100,000 Israelis. "I was a military man for twenty-seven years," he said. "I waged war as long as there was no chance for peace. I believe there is now a chance for peace, a great chance, and we must take advantage of it for those standing here, and for those who are not here—and they are many. I have always believed that the majority of the people want peace and are ready to take a chance for peace."

I do not know how great a chance for peace exists, or if Rabin could have achieved it had he lived to try. Certainly, during my time in the region it was impossible to imagine 100,000 Israelis demonstrating for peace. It would have been difficult to find that many who possessed the faith that peace was within reach. Many Israelis now view Rabin and the peace camp as unwitting contributors to the current bloodshed and view force as the more viable alternative. But Rabin's belief that the majority want peace—whether or not they consider it attainable—remains true, for all sides, and in this I find a measure of hope.

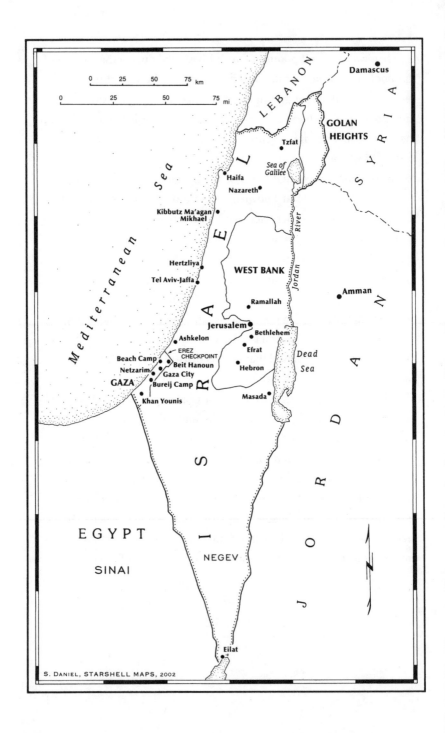

S. DANIEL, STARSHELL MAPS, 2002

Where You Are Standing

Dizengoff Center, Tel Aviv

"**Y**OU'RE IN MY SEAT," I say to the man beside the window. After a long flight to London in an aisle chair and an unexpected ten-hour stopover before boarding my flight to Tel Aviv, I have a non-negotiable appointment with a glass of wine and a window seat.

The man looks up. He is solidly built, bookish, with a pair of steel-rimmed glasses balanced on his nose. "36A?" he asks, feigning confusion.

I look down at my ticket. No, his confusion is not feigned. My ticket reads 35A. I smile apologetically. My impulse is to say I'm sorry, but I remind myself that we're not in Canada any more.

As far as I can tell, I am the only passenger on the flight with no ethnic connection to Israel. Given the spate of violence that started with the eruption of the second intifada in September 2000, and its continued escalation in recent months and days, I am not surprised.

The ultra-Orthodox Jews, or *haredim* ("those who tremble before God"), are the most conspicuous passengers. A number of the men, wearing beards and curling ear locks and dressed in the black suits and hats of eighteenth-century Eastern European Jewry, had been praying earlier in the airport lounge. The women, tutored from an early age to conceal their feminine attributes, shave their heads at marriage and wear a wig or scarf. Their numerous children hide in the folds of their ankle-length skirts.

I spent part of the ten-hour stopover at Heathrow browsing the airport shops. I had time to ponder the judicious placing of the Caviar House, replete with caviar, duck livers, foie gras and champagne, next to the McDonald's. "Any unattended luggage will be removed immediately by police and may be destroyed," a pleasant voice intoned over the loudspeaker. As the two flights to Tel Aviv, scheduled fifteen minutes apart, prepared for boarding, the warning seemed to air at ever tighter intervals. At one point, between additional warnings advising passengers not to agree to watch other people's luggage, a young ultra-Orthodox man approached the middle-aged ultra-Orthodox woman sitting next to me and asked if she would watch his suitcase for a moment. "Of course," she readily agreed. I relocated to a safe distance across the lounge.

On the plane, the ultra-Orthodox passengers make their way to their seats. So near, yet a world away, sit the fashionably dressed secular Israelis clutching shopping bags from Harrods and the airport duty-free shops. When they look at the ultra-Orthodox, their lips visibly tighten. Tensions in Israel between the ultra-Orthodox minority and the secular majority, who label the haredim "fanatics," are second only to those between Arabs and Jews. It is rare for the two groups to be in such close proximity. The tight-knit community of 200,000 ultra-Orthodox Israelis lives in a country apart; they do not share the cultural milieu of mainstream Israeli society, do not read their newspapers, watch their TV shows, shop in their malls or study in their schools. Though the ultra-Orthodox look forward to a messianic future ruled by religious law, their political parties side with any government willing to grant state subsidies to their religious institutions and large families. Secular and moderately religious Israelis resent having their taxes go to support full-time "Torah scholars" who neither serve in the army nor work for a living. Moreover, they resent being dictated to by the increasingly powerful religious parties, whose influence ensures that public transit, stores, restaurants and most everything in the country close down each week for Shabbat.

Rounding out the passengers is a dreadlocked Jewish traveller from North America and a Jewish Canadian high-school girl who has told me she is heading to Jerusalem for a student year abroad. Exceptionally pretty, with long thick hair and a denim skirt, she wears a large Star of David on a chain around her neck.

Since many of the seats on the flight are empty, the man I've mistakenly accused of seat-stealing invites me to sit in his row. Eventually, he even relinquishes the window seat. Saif, it turns out, is an Arab Israeli academic who lectures at Jerusalem's Hebrew University. He is returning from a conference on Palestinian refugees at York University in Toronto. Though Saif's mother tongue is Arabic, he speaks Hebrew equally well. Sometimes better, he confesses. And English, of course. As do most Israelis.

Like many of Israel's more than one million Arab citizens—close to a fifth of the Israeli population—Saif considers himself Palestinian. Israeli Palestinians, as some prefer to call themselves, are in a painfully conflicted position: they are second-class citizens, Arabs in a Jewish state, but citizens nonetheless. They have, until recently, lived at peace with their Jewish neighbours. They still do for the most part, while sympathizing with the suffering of their stateless kin.

It is Saif's belief that the conflict between Israel and Palestinians living under Israeli occupation will not end until the grievances of Palestinian refugees have been addressed. At the very least, he says, Israel must acknowledge its role in their ongoing plight and make a legitimate attempt at recompense. In the civil war of 1948, which broke out after Arabs rejected a United Nations partition plan calling for two states in what was then British Mandate Palestine, some 700,000 Palestinians fled their homes or were forced from them by Israeli armed forces. In 1967, 300,000 Palestinians fled to neighbouring states when Israel occupied the West Bank and Gaza Strip as well as the Golan Heights and the Sinai Peninsula in the Six-Day War. Of these "displaced persons," 120,000 were being uprooted for the second time.

Over the decades, Palestinian refugees have clung to the hope of eventual return. This despite the fact that most of them, numbering almost four million including those in Jordan, Syria and Lebanon, were born and have spent their lives in refugee camps, never having visited the mythical place their parents or grandparents call "home." The right of return is based on a memory, if ameliorated by time, of something better than dislocation, occupation and life in no man's land.

In some ways, Palestinian nationalism is a mirror image of Zionism. Every year at Passover, Jews have prayed that they may celebrate the holiday "next year in Jerusalem." This prayer, repeated through the ages, expressed the desire of those in the Diaspora (the Jewish communities living outside Israel) to return to the Promised Land of their holy books after centuries of absence. When they finally did return, their dream faced a complicated reality: another people was already living there. Indeed, in 1887, all but 5 per cent of the population of historic Palestine—the area between the Mediterranean Sea and the Jordan River—was Arab. In 1920, Palestine came under British rule, and by 1947 immigration had increased the Jewish population sevenfold, to a third of the population, though they owned only 7 per cent of the land. In the wars of 1948 and 1967, it was the indigenous Palestinians who had their societies broken apart, many of them forced into exile. Now, each year, the day after Israelis celebrate Independence Day, Palestinians commemorate their *Nakba*, the day of catastrophe.

Within thirty minutes Saif and I, through our discussions, effectively bring about peace in the Middle East. And the plane has only just taken flight. Now . . . on to the rest of the world's problems.

The flight attendant brings dinner. This is how peace is maintained on international flights: with plenty of mouth-stuffing.

SEVERAL HOURS INTO THE FLIGHT to Tel Aviv, we learn we will be making an unscheduled landing in Cyprus. Why Cyprus? everyone wants to know. As with the flight delay at Heathrow, there is no explanation. When the pilot strolls to the back of the plane, I ask him what's going on. He mumbles something about an order from head office. They must pick up an Israeli crew. The British crew is no longer allowed to stay the night in Tel Aviv due to the "situation." The word "intifada" is not used. Nor are "violence," "suicide bombings" or the latest term for this: "war." As the pilot continues down the aisle, a woman sends sharp words in his direction.

I ask Saif if I should be worried about the so-called situation.

"I am a fatalist," he says. In this, despite a secular university education and an otherwise cosmopolitan outlook, Saif betrays the part of himself that is wholly Middle Eastern. If it is his time to die, it is his time. "You can die anywhere," he says. "You can be hit by a car."

The best solution, he advises, is to avoid following the news.

From my time in the region, I recall Israelis as a newspaper baron's dream demographic (possibly the reason Conrad Black has held on to *The Jerusalem Post* and *The Jerusalem Report* for so long). Wherever there was an Israeli, there was a radio, a TV or some other news source. Even high-school students tuned in to the news. Bus drivers would crank the volume on the radio for the benefit of the passengers, who leaned forward in their seats.

I tell Saif that this time around I want to see as much of Israeli and Palestinian society as I can, to hear as many viewpoints as possible.

"What you see," he says, placing an index finger on either side of his lowered meal tray, "depends on where you are standing."

As we prepare to land in Cyprus, the passengers grow irate. The pilot again announces the brief stop on the public address system, and again manages to avoid any concrete explanation for it. Instead, he apologizes for the confusion and then says, "I would understand if you don't want to fly with us again, but we really hope you will." He adds something about "needing the business." Needing the business? He is clearly unnerved by the passengers' reactions to the unexpected landing. Not that it wasn't scheduled by the airline; our arrival time hasn't changed since we boarded, so they'd obviously factored it in. It simply wasn't mentioned to any of the already apprehensive passengers.

It is dawn as we touch down. Since the passengers have been instructed to stay on the plane, I watch through the window while the crew run head-long across the tarmac, as if the hounds of hell are chasing them.

"They are letting the terrorists know they can take over now," I say.

Saif laughs. And advises me to keep my voice down. "People are very tense," he says. "They will believe you. Look around."

People *are* tense. As soon as we landed, they were out of their seats, disobeying injunctions to wait for a full stop. A subdued anarchy reigns. None of the ultra-Orthodox appear to be praying, but I wonder if now wouldn't be a good time.

To occupy us, Saif teaches me to count in Arabic, then to swear in Hebrew. He teaches me a common Israeli expression: I am so tired my penis is broken. Women also use it, he says.

No doubt it will prove useful, I tell him. After so many hours of travel, it is exactly how I feel.

Next to us, in the aisle seat, a hulking man has slept through most of the flight wearing a powder-blue eye guard. The eye guard looks comical on his enormous head. Now he pushes it up onto his bald pate.

"The fucking British," he says to Saif, referring to the airline staff. "They can go fuck themselves." Saif tells me the man works in Britain. The man told him earlier that the British are nice and well-meaning and easy to manipulate. Heaving himself from his seat, the bald man strides to the back of the plane where the kitchen is located, returning with a coffee. He asks us if we want one, not in a polite way but gruffly, closer to an order than a request, and as though he would as happily dump it on our heads.

"Sure, why not?" I don't risk refusing. Still wearing the eye guard pushed up on his head, the man retreats again to the back of the plane.

The new crew has arrived. We appear to be close to takeoff, but people aren't returning to their seats. Strangers conglomerate, mill about, but there is none of the joyous excitement I have witnessed on previous flights as passengers near the Holy Land. Rather, the energy is one of nervous tension. The new crew seems jumpy, as if they don't quite know how to take control of the situation. The pretty high-school girl is among the most collected of the passengers, kneeling on her seat and reading aloud to her friend from a love letter written by a boy at home.

"He told me he likes a lot of girls," she explains to her companion. "So I said, why bother telling *me* that?" It is clear she has already written him off. He won't be the last to suffer such a fate.

The Israeli hulk returns with our coffee. He tells Saif that the crew informed him there was no coffee left. So he shouted "Café!" and lunged at them. And then there was coffee.

BBC journalist John Simpson, who has travelled to most of the world's dangerous places, has written, "There are three bad times: the night before you leave for somewhere difficult, and you sit with your lover or your family trying to behave entirely normally in order to show how safe everything is going to be; the following morning, when the car comes to take you to the airport; and the moment when the plane touches down at your destination."

Of these, the first two are most difficult for me. Arrival, by contrast, flowers with expectation. As the plane lands in Tel Aviv, my fears and reservations evaporate in the subtropical heat. I have no idea what the future holds. I have moved into the realm of the unpredictable, where all discoveries are made.

I leave Saif in the airport, where I enter the lineup for passengers carrying foreign passports. A waifish ultra-Orthodox youth stands in front of me. He has a long neck and glasses and clutches a large hat box bearing a Brooklyn address in English and Hebrew. When he reaches the front of the line, the young woman at the passport counter barks at him.

"I go today to make a marriage," he tells her, in a nervous accent. He doesn't speak Hebrew or he would have used it. His accent is Yiddish, most likely. There are still communities in Brooklyn that speak Yiddish as their mother tongue.

I am next. She is more polite.

"Do you speak Hebrew?"

"Yes. A little."

"Where are you staying?"

"Hertzliya."

"With whom?"

"With friends."

"Your friend's name?"

I give it.

"Is your friend Jewish?"

"Yes."

A sidelong glance. "Are *you* Jewish?"

"No."

"*Bevakasha.*" If you please.

I pass out of the airport, into close warm air that clutches me to its chest. Like a lover or a captor, I cannot say.

CHAPTER 2

The Same Coin

The Love Parade, Tel Aviv

*I*CAN SEE RIGHT AWAY that I have fallen for it—thinking the Israel I have been watching on TV back in Canada will be the one that exists in reality. In fact, life seems quite normal, almost eerily so.

"Israelis can get used to anything," says Avi. Avi is the son of the Israeli professor whose apartment I'll be based in while I'm here; he and his wife are abroad. We are drinking coffee in the family's kitchen in Hertzliya, an upper-middle-class city a few minutes' drive north of Tel Aviv. Avi tells me there has been an attempted Palestinian suicide bombing every few days over the course of the summer. Some of the bombers are intercepted; others don't succeed in taking any victims (besides themselves) and so don't make the cut for international news. Sporadic bombings aside, life goes on almost as usual, much as I recall it during the Gulf War. In nearby Tel Aviv, that means shopping, cafés, art galleries, nightclubs and the chronic overuse of the cellular phone.

Israelis have one of the highest rates of cell phone use in the world. The phones are a national obsession: the man driving the street sweeper is talking on his (illegally, since drivers are banned from using these menaces) as is the teenaged beauty in skin-tight pants and camouflage tank top whose phone resembles a stuffed puppy dog. Roving packs of eight-year-olds keep their colourful versions strapped to their waistbands so their parents can reach them in the event of an attack. It is common, though it never ceases to surprise me, to see an ultra-Orthodox man holding a miniature cell phone beneath a dangling ear lock. In Israel, old world meets new. As new meets old: many people carry phones in their hands at all times, like technological talismans.

I ask Avi what he considers the biggest change in the country since I last saw him a decade ago. Then, he was just eighteen. Now he's a slim, bespectacled Ph.D. student who wears the Israeli grad student uniform of Bermuda shorts and sandals. He furrows his brow.

"Well, people are richer," he says. "Look around."

The technology boom, while it lasted, was good to Israel, home of the second-largest tech sector in the world after California's Silicon Valley, thanks largely to spin-offs from its formidable military-industrial complex. Everywhere, cars are shiny and new; the prestige sports utility vehicle is edging out more energy-efficient compact models. Air conditioning, once a rarity, has become commonplace. And the first Starbucks recently opened, with plans for another twenty.

The world has come to Israel: from the living room of Avi's parents' apartment, I can tune into BBC, VH-1, MTV, CNN, twenty-four-hour Fashion Television and "I Am Ugly Betty," the wildly popular Colombian soap opera that has its loyal Israeli following picking up Spanish phrases with the assistance of Hebrew subtitles.

One evening, I meet up with Avi and three of his friends, all university-educated, professionally employed Israelis in their mid- to late twenties. We plan to catch a movie, but the film we want to see has only single seats remaining. At the start of the second intifada, many Israelis were avoiding crowded places such as this elegant cinematheque. But people have grown weary of curtailing their lives. We rent a movie from Blockbuster instead.

Avi and his friends all avoid paying too much attention to the news. They live their lives, go to work, travel regularly outside the country. Avi tunes into the evening newscasts only to catch the sports report. He believes the Israeli government is doing all it can to curb the violence. But the government's first priority must be protecting the security of Israelis, not worrying about the impact such security actions may have on Palestinians. Neither is Avi opposed to the targeted executions of Palestinian leaders—"ticking bombs" suspected of planning terrorist acts. At least, he adds, he wouldn't be against them if they were proving effective.

AFTER A FEW DAYS SPENT ACCLIMATIZING, I catch a bus to downtown Tel Aviv to meet Dita Bitterman, one of the founding members of Israel's Women in Black. Nominated for a 2001 Nobel Peace Prize, the group began their weekly vigils a month after the outbreak of the first intifada in 1987. The message they have been repeating for an hour each week, with sporadic breaks when it had seemed their goal was within reach, is inscribed in white letters on the black, hand-shaped signs they carry at vigils and demonstrations: "Stop the Occupation." Solidarity vigils have sprung up around the world, some opposing Israel's continued occupation of the territories, others protesting violence and war in their own countries.

The bus drives past Bauhaus-style apartment buildings, swaying palm trees, and the candy and newspaper mini-marts found on every city block (also the best place, one of Avi's friends has told me, to buy marijuana). At one point, we are caught in heavy traffic. Trapped among the cars, I feel a mounting sense of anxiety. Through the window, I watch a well-dressed, middle-aged man wearing an expensive watch stride toward his car, which is parked directly beside the bus. He has the confident demeanour of someone accustomed to giving orders. The possibility that his car is planted with a bomb is infinitesimal, but I cannot keep from contemplating it.

Be careful and you will be okay, people say. But what is careful? Terrorism works on a lottery system. If you are one of the unlucky winners, you get the windfall. The chances are slim, but everyone who lives here has bought a ticket. Don't go down any dark alleys, advises one of Avi's friends, almost comically. Don't go to East Jerusalem, warns another, adding that of course suicide bombers don't blow themselves up in Arab East Jerusalem—they don't wish to harm their own people.

While waiting for the traffic to clear, I reflect on something Canadian rabbi David Mivasair told me shortly before I left. On a recent trip to Israel, Rabbi Mivasair had accompanied human rights groups on various missions to the occupied territories. He joined Rabbis for Human Rights on a convoy bringing food supplies into the West Bank and, as part of an action planned by the Israeli Committee Against House Demolitions, stayed the night in a Palestinian home slated for demolition. Sometimes, he told me, he wore a baseball cap over his *kipa* (Hebrew for "yarmulke") for added safety, but he never felt directly endangered. I shouldn't worry, he said: given Israel's notorious vehicle mortality rates, I was statistically more likely to die in a traffic fatality than in a terrorist attack.

I get off the bus near Dizengoff Center, a three-storey mall in central Tel Aviv. Malls, conventional wisdom has it, are also to be avoided, though some Israelis find this logic paranoid. Malls have strict security and are almost never targets. But even so . . . It is this helplessness to protect yourself and those you love, the knowledge that you can feel any way you want about the conflict and still be claimed as its victim, that feeds feelings of anger and hate.

The traffic outside the mall is outrageous, as always, with mopeds and pizza delivery scooters driving onto sidewalks or in between vehicle lanes. Cars park wherever they can find a space; an Israeli advertisement for an suv actually uses its ability to park on sidewalks as a selling point. Water delivery trucks stop randomly to unload. Horns blast as drivers vent their frustrations. There are numerous jokes about the Israeli fondness for the horn. Avi had a new one for me. "How do you know that the speed of sound is faster than the speed of light?" "Because you hear the car behind you honking before you see the light turn green."

Dita Bitterman lives on Dizengoff, a once fashionable street now composed mainly of newspaper kiosks and stores selling cheap clothing and dusty tourist souvenirs. She invites me inside her apartment, which is cool and spacious, all white walls and high ceilings. She has cropped hair with a long braided tail at the back. Opposite the living room, in her home office, is a model of her current architectural project, a large white modernist building. There is a slide projector on the dividing wall to the kitchen, the purpose of which will become clear later on.

She makes strong coffee—filtered, a welcome change from the Israeli preference for instant—and we settle in to talk about her peace work. Bitterman is involved with the Coalition of Women for a Just Peace, an umbrella organization that represents nine Israeli and Palestinian women's peace groups. As part of her work, she joins other Israeli activists on food and water convoys into the occupied territories. When she speaks about her motivations, she becomes focussed and intense.

"We've been educated to be afraid and paranoid of the Arabs," she says. "The Israelis push the Palestinians into a corner so they can't see any way out. If you can't see any hope, you become more radical. You have nothing to lose. To fight to the death, it's not only the death of Palestinians but of Israelis, too. Palestinians are without water, not to mention freedom. Israel must understand it. They will understand it the hard way."

The groups she works with have a different agenda: to lower

suspicions, to promote understanding and respect, to realize a long-term vision that involves co-existence. I mention the widely held view that Israelis are doing everything they can to bring about peace, that Palestinian leaders rejected Israel's best offer at Camp David.

She is familiar with this mainstream perspective. "Why should Israelis think otherwise?" she says. "It diminishes their standard of living." The truth is that Palestinians were offered a large proportion of land but not a viable state. "The West Bank map was like Swiss cheese with a lot of Israeli settlements." She adds that many settlers are in the occupied territories not for religious reasons but for the favourable real estate prices.

"The Israelis on the right claim the Palestinians have twenty-two countries," says Bitterman. "We, the Jewish, have only one state in the world. We were deported from elsewhere. Why don't they leave? We have an answer for this. The Palestinians live here as much as the Jews. They have the same father. It's at least as much their land as ours."

Bitterman grew up on a kibbutz, one of the model Israeli communities dedicated to achieving a kind of socialist utopia—and one of the only places in the world where that goal has enjoyed a measurable success. There, she says, she was educated to believe in justice and fairness for all. She was "naïve enough" to believe such ideals were realistic. "Most Israelis are afraid to take this point of view," she says. Her family considers her an extremist.

"The Israeli point of view derives from a military point of view," she explains. "We have a history of militant education. We were taught we were a nation under siege. So you develop a strategy. You learn to fight back, to not give an inch. The military education is to solve problems in the short term."

Bitterman was one of ten women in Tel Aviv who began gathering in public areas in 1987 to demonstrate against the occupation. They started on Dizengoff Street, bringing a projector and showing slides of Palestinians being beaten in the occupied territories. The reactions on the street, she says, were "very violent."

The women were undaunted. They connected with women's groups that had started simultaneously in Haifa and Jerusalem. The result was like "mushrooms after the rain," Bitterman says. They adopted an approach modelled on Argentina's Mothers of the Disappeared, who demonstrate wearing black and carrying photographs of their missing loved ones. Before long, women were gathering at as many as thirty-nine locations throughout the country. Because of the simplicity of the message, women of differing viewpoints could find common ground. Later, through consensus, certain vigils adopted additional slogans like "Negotiations with the PLO," at a time when this option was not only radical but illegal.

"People tend to see two sides to the coin," she says finally, "but it's the same coin. Me and you."

YESTERDAY, FOUR BOMBS—all in Jerusalem.

I spend the day in Tel Aviv. The Carmel Market near Allenby Street beckons: packed, noisy, full of sharp smells and of vendors singing the virtues of their green grapes or hawking pirated CDs, old women and men with their shopping carts, girl soldiers trying on earrings, piles of charms to ward off the evil eye, and the world's most perfect foods— tomatoes, hummus, fresh pita, feta cheese. But I am avoiding crowded places, so I skirt through the side alleys, past the butcher shops where enormous slabs of meat—half an animal at a time—are being trans- ported on supermarket grocery carts. Plucked chickens hang from the open-air stalls by their legs. The men behind the counters call out to me to take their photographs until I run out of film.

I have lunch at a place called Roni Fuul, a frenetic cafeteria-style eatery. The servers plunk down onto the table a bowl of raw onion with a dipping sauce, then drop felafel onto your plate with their hands, bringing more and more until you plead with them to stop. You pay only for the amount you eat.

One of the servers is a wiry, energetic Israeli, quick on his feet, who makes conversation when he's not responding to demands from impatient customers. He tells me he speaks six languages and owns an apartment in Amsterdam. He can't take the winters there, though. Too cold. Where else but in Israel, I wonder, does your waiter speak six languages and own property abroad?

I pay the cashier for my salad and felafel and walk a few blocks farther to Jaffa. The four-thousand-year-old port city, now swallowed up by the Tel Aviv municipality, was the largest Arab city in Palestine before it was conquered by Jewish forces on the eve of Israel's declaration of independence. The beautiful stone houses the refugees abandoned became housing for new Jewish immigrants. They are now some of the most coveted real estate in the country.

Resting for a moment on a bench beneath a palm tree, I am approached by a young man carrying a motorcycle helmet.

"You have seen someone waiting here?" he asks.

I haven't.

"I am late," he shrugs. "It happens sometimes."

His name is Yossi. He is an acupuncturist. Business isn't great, he says. Israelis are very traditional. It takes time for them to accept a new approach.

Yossi wears his long hair pulled back in a ponytail. He would be handsome if not for a mouthful of yellowed teeth. I ask him how he feels about the "situation."

"I don't give a damn about the Arabs," he says, first off. He thinks they had their chance for a peace agreement and blew it. "They want the whole country, but we live here, too." He thinks Israel needs to "conquer" the occupied territories again. Send in the troops. But it is not long before he contradicts himself.

"They are human, we are human. We all deserve to live. I don't want this—the army, the military service."

He is twenty-nine, and served his three years of army duty in the West Bank town of Ramallah. He didn't like it. He says he would rather live and work with Arabs than fight them.

"You want that you can stay here and I can move to Canada?" he suggests. All he would like is the opportunity to wake up in the morning and go to work and never be forced to think about the "situation" again.

"Do you go to full-moon parties?" he asks, changing the subject. These are outdoor raves where young people gather during the full moon to dance, smoke pot, take ecstasy—forget. The last full-moon party he went to, the DJ had been flown in from Japan. The police busted the entire group, and a girl he knows was arrested for carrying a joint. "The organizers lost a lot of money," he says. As he is telling me this, a police van drives past, caught in the slow-moving traffic. He follows it with his eyes.

He considers revealing the location of the next full-moon party but concludes, "I don't know you."

"I'm not a cop," I say.

"I know that," he says, "but you might *call* the cops."

Last summer, he was driving his motorcycle along the waterfront of Tel Aviv, not far from where we are sitting, when he came upon a mass of police cars and flashing lights. It was late, and a large number of young people had congregated at the side of the road, talking on their cell phones. He called his girlfriend, who told him there had been a bomb.

"It was at the Dolphinarium. You have heard of it?" Yossi asks.

The Dolphinarium is the discotheque where twenty-one Israelis, most of them teenaged immigrants from Russia, were killed in a bloody suicide bombing that rocked the country. I and millions of people around the world had heard of it.

Leaving Yossi to wait for his friend, I head to Sheinkin Street, the central shopping district in Tel Aviv. Shops there range from designer clothing boutiques to body-piercing parlours to the Kabbalah store filled with mystical books, jewellery and bottled Kabbalah water. At the cafés, it is impossible to find a seat. The tables extend onto the sidewalks. Young Israeli men in baggy nylon pants and tank tops keep a wolfish eye on the passing young women, who believe, when it comes to fashion, that tighter is better and less is more. The bands of armed soldiers taking an afternoon stroll are so common they become part of the scenery. It is almost possible to forget that it's a year into the worst fighting this generation has ever seen.

I stop in at a cramped boutique called the Empress, where a saleswoman named Sharon tries to interest me in the latest dresses by Yosef, a popular Israeli designer. A tall Israeli blonde emerges from the changeroom in a denim hoop skirt, and twirls.

Sharon, petite with a head of wild curls, is an artist recently returned from three years in Los Angeles. She tells me that there aren't any tourists in Israel right now. "It's really bad," she says. "Hotels are closing. People are out of work."

Her male co-worker, tall with a strong jaw, sniffs at this remark. "We don't need tourists," he says, sounding offended. "It's not dangerous here. If they want danger, they can go to Croatia." With this, he storms out of the store.

"How are people coping?" I ask Sharon. Her co-worker has already provided one answer.

"The new generation doesn't want this," she says. "Israelis travel a lot. After the army"—three years of mandatory service for men, twenty-one months for women—"we go to the Far East. To Australia. To America. In the past, in our parents' generation, people were willing to make sacrifices. But this generation sees that other people don't live this way. Other people don't have to go into the army. It's not normal. We want to have normal lives. So this generation doesn't watch the news. We try to ignore it. Even with the suicide bombings, I still go out. I won't change my life for this. You know yesterday"— by yesterday, she means the bombings in Jerusalem—"when I was going home, everyone was out. The restaurants and cafés were full."

"It's absurd," she says, of the situation. "This is not a way to live. It's absurd."

Later that afternoon, I learn there has been another suicide bombing in Jerusalem. The news report says the bomber was disguised as ultra-Orthodox. When people reported suspicions to a pair of police officers, the police approached the man, who then detonated himself. Twenty-one were wounded, one seriously. The bomber was just blocks from the Sbarro pizzeria, ground zero of an earlier, deadlier suicide bombing. The bomber's blood and flesh splashed across cars and people. He was outside the French International School, where many foreign journalists send their children (as do many Arabs). It was 7:45 a.m., the time when parents were dropping off their children. His head rolled into the school yard.

THE ANNUAL LOVE PARADE IN TEL AVIV takes up the entire waterfront. Thirteen floats were contributed by Israeli nightclubs, which have suffered a decline in attendance since the bombing at the Dolphinarium. No one seems averse to crowds today. Loudspeakers blast house and techno music for tens of thousands of Israeli ravers (organizers claim there are 300,000, and it certainly feels that way) who sport body paint, G-strings, antennae, dreadlocks, faux-fur legwarmers and plenty of hormones. They are guarded by the lucky soldiers whose assignment it is that day; some of the soldiers groove in the street, M-16s slung from their backs.

An area of about twenty square blocks is cordoned off for the parade. It would seem like life as usual, MTV-style, except for the lineups to have your bags checked when you enter the area and the news report of another shooting today, by a Palestinian dressed as a soldier. And this: walking down a back street to avoid the punishing crowds, I come upon an egg-shaped man in a kipa and dark John Lennon glasses. I recognize him from the market, where he was pushing a cart covered with religious bumper stickers and passing out pamphlets. This time, his cart is positioned in front of a synagogue, and he has set out speakers blasting Hebrew songs at full volume. His poor cart won't be attracting any of the purple G-string club kids, though, unless it has a supply of ecstasy inside.

I walk back up to the market and sit on a cement bench to eat my dinner: felafel and hummus in a pita. Three soldiers are standing nearby, guarding the entrance to the market. I often doubt the effectiveness of the security presence—so many of the bag checks are no more than a cursory fumble—so I am pleased to see that these three are paying attention; the one in black-framed glasses even checks the trash bin near my bench for a bomb. After a time, a guy sitting close by strikes up a conversation. His name is Oren, he tells me. He is a thirty-two-year-old accountant with a shaved head who studied at Tel Aviv University the same year I did. He acknowledges that he is one of the last Israelis not to own a cell phone. He is holding out, he says, because he doesn't want his employers to be able to call him outside of office hours.

"Life is very hard in Israel," he says. "People are anxious. That's why they are so aggressive. That's why they are always in a hurry, honking their horns." In the background, the evening traffic bears out his words. This is also why he is leaving for Australia next month. If he can find work, he doesn't plan to return.

Oren says Israelis are thinkers, perhaps more so than the citizens of any other country. I'm not sure there's any data to support his claim, but it is true that Israeli academics publish more scientific papers per capita than academics elsewhere, and that Israel has more physicians and engineers per capita, too. It's also true that, once you've been here awhile, there's a hell of a lot to think about.

CHAPTER 3

The Air You Breathe

Women in Black, Haifa

*I*WATCH THE TWO ISRAELI teenagers slumped on a bench in the shade at a bus stop in Hertzliya. The girl, wearing a Superman T-shirt, takes out her cell phone and runs through every possible ringer option. There must be twenty. Her boyfriend listens to each electronic tune from under a mop of unruly hair and passes mumbled judgement. "Lo. Lo. Lo." None of them makes the cut.

Between a bus and a shared taxi driven by an Arab Israeli who once worked as a chef in a French restaurant—the stress was bad for his heart, he says, hence the career change—I make the hour-long journey north to Nazareth. Nazareth is a dusty, sunburned town of low white houses with a mixed Jewish and Arab population. I make my way to the Arab section, home to both Christians and Muslims, and spend a few minutes looking through a jumbled clothing shop and a United Colors of Benetton store that stands empty save for sales staff, its message of cultural harmony not attracting any customers today. I have made a point of wearing long pants and a long-sleeved shirt in deference to the local culture, but the women in the shops clearly favour miniskirts and high heels. At a small grocery store I buy an apple; the young Arab man at the cash register insists on washing it for me before he will let me take it.

At the recently opened Howard Johnson hotel, where I stop to take advantage of the air conditioning, three Arab Israelis stand outside talking. Inside, the lobby is as still as a sarcophagus, no indents on the overstuffed Louis xiv–style chairs. I am halfway across the gleaming floor before an apologetic security guard catches up to me and politely asks to check my bag: just standard protocol, checking for bombs or weapons.

Evidently, it has been a long time since the security guard has seen any tourists in this pilgrims' destination, thought to have been home to Mary, Joseph and the baby Jesus. Legend has it that Nazareth was also home to the region's most beautiful women, all of them, unfortunately for their admirers, related to the Virgin. In the souvenir case near the vacant check-in desk are a selection of men's ties commemorating the millennium; a collector's plate of Jesus wearing a crown of thorns, his eyes rolled toward the ceiling; and some carved olive-wood doves, symbols of peace that nobody is buying.

I am in Nazareth to meet Nabila Espanioly, an Arab Israeli peace activist and the director of the local women's centre. Espanioly is a founding member of the Women in Black in the port city of Haifa, where she lived before moving to Nazareth. She is one of several Arab Israelis active in the primarily Jewish vigil.

The women's centre is located down a dusty alleyway. In the unadorned reception area, a young woman types a Microsoft Word document in Arabic script, then switches to Hebrew. Hanging from a bulletin board is an Internet printout popular among feminist news-groups, which notes that Marilyn Monroe was a size 14 and that most women report feeling depressed and insecure after two minutes spent looking at a fashion magazine. Beside the printout is a picture of a baby wearing a T-shirt that reads, "I don't know left from right, but I know I have the right of return."

Espanioly welcomes me into the room where she has just concluded a meeting. She is a substantial woman whose curly hair has the colour and luminescence of crude oil, but her presence is larger than her physique. We sit in a library surrounded by children's books and teaching aids used to promote gender-neutral education in the local Arab schools.

"Sitting here and witnessing what's happening, it's destroying me," says Espanioly. "I'm so depressive in these times, when I know that I can't change the issues."

The Women in Black vigils, she explains, started as a way for women, who often have little free time between career and family, to make their views known. A one-hour commitment at the same time each week was something most women could manage. At first, Espanioly wanted the vigils to express more than a demand to end the occupation. She has views, strong opinions. Then she saw the logic of a simple platform that allowed for broad consensus.

Coping with reactions on the street was another matter.

"They were calling us names like Arab-fuckers and Arab-lovers," she says, describing responses to early vigils held in Haifa. Most of the comments were directed less at the women's message than at their gender. Standing on street corners on Friday afternoons, they were often told, "Go and cook your meals for Shabbat." On one occasion, right-wing counter-demonstrators showed up and burned an effigy of Arafat.

"That day it was very violent and I was struggling not to shout, not to answer, because we were supposed to be silent," recalls Espanioly. "I didn't want to cry in front of them." One of the most painful remarks was directed at an eighty-year-old doctor, a devoted Woman in Black who had survived the Holocaust. "She had a number on her arm. People could see that she was a survivor. Someone said, 'It's too bad that Hitler didn't finish with you.'"

To keep a step ahead of the counter-demonstrators, the women started changing locations each week, phoning each other with the new address shortly before the designated time. Today, Espanioly isn't sure the Women in Black have any effect. The media ignores them. The overall number of peace activists in Israel has dropped precipitously, such that she thinks there may now be only 3,000 left in all the country. But at least these vigils and other peace activities keep the issues on the table, she says. And help her keep her sanity.

Though the Women in Black vigils bring together Jewish and Arab Israelis, the conflict has deepened the rift in the greater society. Espanioly has experienced it first-hand. Due to a real estate shortage in the Arab area of Nazareth, she owns an apartment in the Jewish area. One night near the beginning of the current intifada, she awoke to the sound of voices shouting, "Death to Arabs. Death to Arabs." She went to the window. Hundreds of young Jewish Israelis were gathered outside in their cars. She flicked on the light, then snapped it off, fearing she might attract their attention.

The next day she took the elevator down from her apartment with a Jewish neighbour clad in military fatigues. She told him what had occurred during the night. "These are just crazy people," he told her. He said he hadn't heard a thing.

"And on my way here I was thinking, why should he hear it? He is not threatened by their presence. In Israel, they say, 'Never again.' But it doesn't mean never again for humanity, never again for everyone. It means never again for the Jews."

Does all this make her angry? I ask.

"It makes me furious. It makes me angry. It makes me afraid. My anger normally I translate into action, but I'm in a situation today, concerning what's happening in the West Bank and Gaza, mainly, where I am helpless. This is me, who is normally very optimistic, who is normally full of energy for action. But today, what positive action can I do? I mean against assassinations, against killing. And the language—you have just to hear the language; they decide on the death penalty for Palestinians without any trial, without any hearing, and they call it protection of Israel, defence for Israel! It makes me angry? It makes me furious! And this is my fear. If I allow my feelings to come out I don't know what will happen. I'll explode.

"Then they ask how people have come to bomb themselves. I mean, when life doesn't have any meaning any more, when life means only waiting for the next disaster and the next disaster is at my window or at my door, then what can I do?

"I think that many Israelis don't know what's happening in the West Bank and Gaza. They don't know and they don't want to know."

She talks about the "art of survival" developing in the West Bank and Gaza, and wonders how long it can last. She doesn't believe Israel will succeed in crushing the Palestinians. "The time for destroying a people is over," she says. "Hitler tried, and he wasn't able to succeed. So if Hitler didn't succeed in all that, no one will succeed. It's over. It's over. I hope."

She sees attempts to put down the Palestinian revolt as counterproductive. To illustrate her point, she tells the story of a fourteen-year-old boy who lost his feet in the first intifada. He was interviewed in 2000, shortly after the outbreak of the second uprising.

"He's the oldest son in the family and he's working by selling fruit in the morning and in the afternoon he goes for demonstrations against the soldiers. And they were asking him, 'Aren't you afraid?' and he said, 'Of what?' 'Of death.' 'But how will that be different from our life?' It has come to that, that death means hope. Death is becoming hope for many. When you believe that when you are dead you will have heaven, and heaven is the only hope that you have, then why not die? It's better than life."

After our meeting, I walk to the Arab market in Nazareth. The streets are filled with Arab students returning from school, most of them wearing school uniforms. The market used to attract many Jewish customers who came for the atmosphere and good prices, but as the conflict has deepened, they have stopped coming. It seems the more that dialogue is needed, the more the unstructured opportunities to practise co-existence disappear.

Passing a plain-looking mosque, I decide to step inside. A young man gets up from talking to his friends to show me around. I expect him to request money for acting as my guide, but the subject never arises. He points to the chandeliers, cheap modern fixtures of gold-painted metal, and we admire them together. I leave and wander the winding market streets alone, past stalls peopled with more shopkeepers than shoppers. No one calls out to me, tries to encourage me to buy, except one young boy of ten or eleven who speaks to me in Hebrew. "Lady," he shouts, "lady," clowning for attention.

I stop at the Basilica of the Annunciation, run by the Franciscans. It is an imposing structure, rather modern in its austere flat lines, built in the 1960s. Arab workers are busy inside, pounding away at the stones around the grotto where legend has it that Mary was first told by the angel Gabriel that God had made her pregnant. A thin trickle of tourists, the first I've seen today, busy themselves with their Handycams. Outside, in the garden, is the real photo op: an elderly Franciscan in a simple brown robe who cuts a handful of white roses, then, with limping gait, takes them to place next to the grotto.

On my way out, I peer into a room next to the front gate, startling the Arab security guard. He has a friendly face, and invites me to sit down. He looks to be in his mid-fifties, my father's age.

"Are you Christian?" he asks me. In the West, discussing religion or politics doesn't qualify as small talk. Here, it is the air you breathe.

"No."

"Jewish?"

"No."

"What then?"

"Nothing," I tell him.

"You can't be nothing."

I stall for a few moments, then let him off the hook.

"Well, my parents are Christian."

Aaah . . .

He himself was raised Catholic. "I studied to be a priest, but it was hard, too hard. It's not normal." He shakes his head. "Not normal." He says he knew one Franciscan brother who had a lady friend outside. "It's necessary," he says. He himself quit the priesthood and got married. He has two children, a girl and a boy, both grown.

"The brothers serve here three years," he says. "Like the army."

I ask if he is still a Catholic.

"I believe," he says, "but not like the brothers. They believe God is only good. But I see little children, bad things happen to them. I say, how can this be a good God?"

He still prays every day. But he harbours reservations. "Maybe God is a woman," he says. "Who knows?"

The guard's son is getting a Master's degree in computer science. In Toronto. The young man wants to remain in Canada. "In Israel, if my son wants a job in computers, they will first choose the Jew. Maybe if he knows someone he will find a place. In Canada, he tells me, people don't ask you what religion you are."

Later, on the main road, I buy a demitasse of strong coffee from a man sitting on the sidewalk next to a large brass samovar. Arab schoolchildren jostle at bus stops, the boys showing off for the girls. A bus passes carrying only Muslim women in headscarves. In the entire day, I see one man in a kipa.

I find the bus stop for Haifa and wait on a bench between an Arab in a wool suit jacket, with a dirty moustache, slurred speech and suspiciously red eyes, and an Arab girl wearing jeans—she is Christian, most likely, since Christian women favour a pointedly Western style of dress—who tells me which bus to take. When it pulls in, the driver, a svelte Middle Eastern Tom Jones with lustrous curls of jet-black hair and tight pants, steps out to talk to some friends.

I climb into the bus and sit down. A young man who looks barely old enough to shave, much less drive, slips into the driver's seat. Tom Jones, when he gets back on the bus, takes the first seat behind the driver, across the aisle from where I am sitting.

The new driver pulls out the ticket dispenser gingerly, as if it's the first time he's handled it. Before long, I begin to suspect it is. He is handsome and lean in his T-shirt and jeans. In the rearview mirror, his dark eyes gleam with excitement. No one else gets on the bus. Finally, we pull out onto the road. I still haven't been asked to buy a ticket.

Tom Jones leans back in his seat, puts his feet up and makes a call on his cell phone. I can hear a woman's voice on the other end. Every so often, the young driver shouts out his contribution to their conversation from behind the wheel. When the conversation ends, the phone rings again. Tom talks for a while, obviously enjoying himself, then signals to me that he needs to borrow my pen and a piece of paper. He uses them to jot down a phone number. It appears the second caller is also female.

Another bus passes, heading in the opposite direction. The bus driver lays on the horn, waving excitedly at the other driver. When he stops to pick up a passenger, he asks Tom how much to charge.

Later on, Tom returns my pen. When we start talking, I learn that both drivers are Bedouin. Both did army service, then? Yes, they say with pride, three years. Bedouins serve in the Israeli military, like the Druze (who follow an offshoot of Islam) and Jewish Israelis.

The Bedouin are good trackers, aren't they? I ask.

Yes, they say, pleased that their reputation precedes them, but adding, Not any more. These are city Bedouin, good at following the road. Or so I hope.

The bus driver wants to know if I am Christian.

No, I tell him.

Jewish?

No.

Confusion reigns.

"Do you believe?" asks the driver, trying another tack.

"I don't believe," I say.

His brow wrinkles. This clearly distresses him, so I attempt, in the Hebrew that is a second or third language to all three of us, to explain. "I believe in something, something bigger than me. I don't know exactly what."

It is enough to give comfort. The driver smiles, relieved, into the rearview mirror, revealing a row of white teeth. He believes, he assures me. I take the opportunity to hand him my bus fare. He is sheepish, realizing he should have asked for it earlier, but he does a competent job of making change. He's getting the hang of this now.

Tom Jones, whose name is actually Taleb, wants to add my phone number to the list he's been compiling. I counter that he is a busy man with a big phone bill. He needs a book, not just a scrap of paper. In the end he settles for giving me his cell number. I doubt I could get through if I tried.

That evening, I have dinner with Jewish friends in Haifa. They are an educated couple in their early thirties—a physicist and a lawyer—with a delightful four-year-old daughter. I tell them about meeting Nabila Espanioly, about the Arab security guard, the Bedouin drivers.

The physicist tells me I'm naïve. "Arabs only understand force," he says. When I challenge his generalization (he does not, himself, know any Arabs), he says, "You are too Swiss. You need to choose the side you are on." He and his wife no longer go to Nazareth. They are afraid to— with their young daughter, even more so.

That night, sleeping in their spare room, I awaken to the distant strains of music floating in through the open window. The music resembles the Muslim call to prayer, as sorrowful and sweet, and I feel a deep sense of sadness pass through me. The next day, a news report. A bomb found on the main road from Nazareth. It was detonated before it could explode.

CHAPTER 4

This Heated Place

Staircase to the Western Wall, Jerusalem

*T*HE JERUSALEM BUS station is new. The old central station was a dilapidated place; I recall several occasions on past visits when everyone in the station was evacuated while a suspicious package was examined or destroyed.

Canadian writer Mordecai Richler had a brush with this "better safe than sorry" policy when he arrived in Israel in 1992 and accidentally left his new Smith Corona XD 5500 electric typewriter on a cart in the airport parking lot. The director of the guest house where he was staying made enquiries and reported back. "I've got good news and bad news for you," she told him. "The good news is that they found your typewriter. The bad news is that they blew it up."

Since then, the security precautions have risen exponentially. Every bus now passes though a security gate, each passenger through an individual security check. The newspaper *Ha'aretz* notes that nearly 10 per cent of the Israeli work force is now employed in some form of security. I join the throngs of passengers pushing single file into the station, but I haven't yet learned to keep my elbows out, so I am shuffled to the end of a long queue.

The guard takes a moment to assess me. "You have a gun?" he asks.

"A what?"

"A gun."

This must be a tactic he learned in security-guard school. No, no gun.

The new bus station is rather like the new Times Square: shiny, Disney-fied, devoid of the roughness and filth that gave its predecessor character. The bright, open-concept stores are filled with high fashion at high prices. There is a McDonald's and a "crêperie." At the espresso bar I order a coffee but receive a latté. Unlike the old stone station, this place aspires to membership in the Material World. If not for the large numbers of armed soldiers waiting to be bussed to their posts, I could be in any mall in any city in North America.

With exceptions. In the weeks since the new station opened its doors, ultra-Orthodox leaders have already succeeded in delaying the opening of the McDonald's, and have forced the lingerie shop to tone down its window display and the Internet café to change its screensavers. They have also, by starting a pirate bus line that separates men from women, convinced the national bus service, Egged, to operate special segregated runs for them at discounted ticket prices. A parliament member from Shinui—a party that won six seats in the last election on a platform that states, essentially, "We will fight the haredim"—has threatened to take the issue to Israel's High Court. "Egged is turning the central bus station into a *haredi* ghetto," the Shinui member told reporters. "From now on we have to change the name from Egged Lines to Taliban Lines."

I board a bus that winds through the crowded New City. Through the window I watch a lanky Hasidic youth bound across Jaffa Street in a few long strides. The Hasidim are a mystical ultra-Orthodox sect that originated in Eastern Europe, and the young man wears a suit and a large fur hat fit for a Polish winter, on a day when the temperature will surpass thirty degrees. At the entrance to the Old City, I follow a similar black-hatted young man through Jaffa Gate.

Once inside the Old City, I feel instantly calmed. The ancient walls of milky Jerusalem stone stand impervious to time and to the streams of humanity who live out their lives within these confines. The walls do not complain, nor do they suffer complaints. They will see this generation and the next as they have seen the many who came before them. The knowledge is oddly comforting.

The Arab market, housed in a series of narrow corridors covered to blunt the punishing sun, is crammed with shops selling every kind of souvenir. "Come look." "Just a moment." "Where are you from?" Each shopkeeper tries out his arsenal of persuasive lines in a litany of languages. The shopkeepers are primarily Muslim, but wallets of all faiths are welcomed. You want a menorah? A silver cross? An Israeli army baseball cap?

"Business is slow," I comment to a weary-looking vendor who reclines on a stool outside his T-shirt store.

"Not slow," he says, making no effort to get up, or even to look up. "Dead."

I find the Lutheran Hospice around the corner from the market. It is run by those for whom, it appears, cleanliness is next to godliness, which to any traveller is a tenet that almost merits conversion. It is a lovely place with high stone walls and a quiet garden with a lily pond and tables at which to sit and write. In the cavernous downstairs are thirty bunk beds for women travellers. Only a handful are occupied.

Stirring in the bunk bed next to the one I've been assigned is a young Australian named Candace. She is pretty in a studious, Jane Goodall kind of way: no makeup, long hair pulled back in a braid. She warns me to watch out for the crusading Pentecostals who stay here, tracts and Bibles at the ready. Candace is twenty-four and has just finished her Ph.D. thesis on "American Policy towards Jerusalem and the Occupied Territories from 1948 to 1967." Has anything changed since then?

"Nothing," she says.

She also reports that she recently heard an explosion nearby but figures it was only a bomb being detonated by the army. Nothing to be concerned about, she assures me.

CONFLICT IS THE LEITMOTIF OF this heated place. What is today the state of Israel has at various times been controlled by Canaanites, Israelites, Assyrians, Babylonians, Persians, Greeks, Egyptians, Romans, Arabs, Turks and the British. The tectonic plates of half the world's religions collide here, push up against one another until the pressure forces the geography of power to change—an eruption, subduction, earthquake; the birth of a new mountain range from what was once an ocean floor.

"There will be a war here," says Mikael, a polite Armenian doctoral student who resides at the hospice while studying at Hebrew University. He has taken a private room, and I often find him in the communal kitchen, cooking. Does he believe this for political or religious reasons?

"Both political and religious," he decides.

As always, the two cannot be pried apart.

I spend a morning taking photographs in the Old City. The Jerusalem Organization of Kitsch Souvenir Sellers must have given a weekend workshop on the Seven Skills of Highly Annoying Vendors, because they seem to have stepped up their sales offensives. A Palestinian man follows me into the silent Franciscan chapel where I have taken refuge and tries to sell me a guide to the *via dolorosa*. I know now why the route bears that name—Jesus had to both carry the cross *and* fend off the vendors who wanted to sell him a piece of it. "Listen," I want to say, "would I follow you into Al-Aksa mosque and try to sell you a guide to the Haram ash-Sharif?" Instead, I pretend to be deep in prayer.

More and more I see how this city survives by sucking every red cent out of stupefied pilgrims. Economically, since the intifada decimated tourism, the vendors are at the point of eating their own flesh. The only Westerners left are aid workers and journalists. Tourists are so rare in the current environment that everyone wants a piece of me.

Back at the hospice, Mikael invites me to join him and two of his Armenian friends in the rooftop garden for some of his homemade borscht. It's the best offer I've had all day. One of his friends, Gregor, works for the United Nations Special Coordinator in Gaza City. The other, John, works for a multinational accounting firm on a U.S. Agency for International Development (USAID) project in the West Bank.

We sit outside, eating borscht and drinking red wine. Church bells peal around us.

Mikael perks up his ears. "That is the Greek," he says.

Moments later, a different set of bells. "That is the Latin."

Over the course of the meal, Mikael identifies two or three more. He studies Armenian manuscripts, but he is well acquainted with Christian liturgy and the iconography of all denominations. He calls the Bible-thumping Pentecostals who flit about the hospice, playing guitar and speaking in tongues, "pagans."

"Why are there Jews and Muslims crossing here?" asks Gregor, looking out from the garden to the rooftop opposite, where a steady stream of men in black suits and hats are walking to and fro. Occasionally, a Palestinian crosses their path.

"We are at the centre of the four quarters," says Mikael. "There is the Muslim," he points, "there the Jewish, there the Christian, there the Armenian."

I mention hearing the Muslim call to prayer coincide with the sound of church bells earlier in the day.

"You are sure it wasn't an F-16?" asks Gregor jokingly.

"It was louder than an F-16," I say. During times of tension, I've heard that the volume on the pre-recorded calls to prayer is turned up.

The borscht lacks beets and potatoes, but it is good enough for these homesick Armenians. We drink more wine, eat thick chewy bread, and savour the meal because someone else has made it and we are all together with no one trying to sell us anything.

After dinner, I sit in the quiet of the garden. An older German traveller named Hans comes outside to join me. He offers to share from two brown paper bags filled with almonds and dates. Twilight falls, and we watch the silhouettes of the ultra-Orthodox heading to prayers.

Tomorrow, Hans plans to visit a priest he knows in the West Bank. "But I don't tell my wife," he confides. He will tell her after he returns safely.

Jerusalem, he says, is the centre of the world. He's right: on medieval maps, cartographers marked it as the centre of the universe. I tell him that where we are sitting, at the crux of the four quarters, is the precise epicentre. We are silent for a while, watching the passing show.

"I was here twenty years ago," he says, "and there were Muslims praying all through here, but now I see only Jewish." He pauses for a moment. "What I cannot believe is that the Jewish can be to the Palestinians as Hitler was to the Jewish."

It begins to rain. A set of church bells, which Mikael would recognize but I do not, rings out. Followed by another. And another.

ON MY WAY BACK TO THE HOSPICE one afternoon, a French-speaking Hasid wearing a fur hat and a black silk caftan that looks like a smoking jacket starts up a conversation. At first I am pleased to have the opportunity to speak to him. It is difficult to engage the ultra-Orthodox; their communities are closed to outsiders, particularly non-Jews, and even more so to women. I feel disappointed when I catch on to his line of questioning: How long are you here, where is your hotel, would you like to meet me in an hour?

The Old City of Jerusalem is among the world's worst locations for a one-night stand: everyone who lives within this square kilometre will see one another again. But as a traveller, I will be gone soon. The man can tell from my appearance that I am probably not Jewish, and so his actions, if he gets away with them, are "okay." Within his community's strictures, or at least not quite so far outside them. He is nice about the proposition, and I am nice about it, too, but not *that* nice. We part ways; he follows one of the myriad winding stone passages and I never see him again.

In the evening Candace and I walk through the pedestrian mall in West Jerusalem. Young ultra-Orthodox men are dancing feverishly in the open square, carrying yellow flags that read "Messiah." They hold out the belief that the Messiah is arriving right now, in this very moment. When we pass back through, hours later, they are still dancing, and one of them has commandeered a microphone. The Messiah hasn't joined them yet.

Candace and I find an outdoor patio restaurant. It is a cool Jerusalem night, but the kerosene burners have been lit to keep us warm. Most of the customers are young lovers. Israelis are not drinkers, and we are among the few who order a glass of wine. As time passes, the patio becomes crowded. I begin to feel uneasy. It is too busy; people are too unaware of their surroundings, immersed in their conversations, not watchful or guarded. It's the kind of atmosphere that would appeal to a suicide bomber.

"It's too open for a suicide bomber," says Candace. "They want a closed space."

I start to laugh. These are the things we tell ourselves, the rationale that keeps the fear at bay. "Suicide bombers aren't necessarily known for the wisdom of their planning process," I reply. Avi has told me that he often considers, in the aftermath of a suicide bombing, the bomber's ineptitude, and how he himself might have done better.

A few days later, a Friday, I walk to the Western Wall around sunset. At the entrance, I pass through a metal detector and open my bag for a security guard. A young yeshiva student rushes past, flashing a card that allows him to circumvent the formal search. Like many of the worshippers, he carries his submachine gun with him.

The Western Wall, the remnant of a retaining wall built by Herod the Great around the Second Temple compound, is impressive in its banality. It is nothing but flat stone, furrowed with cracks into which supplicants stuff prayers scrawled on scraps of paper. Men and women have separate sections at the Wall. Some of the men wear the black suits and hats of the ultra-Orthodox. Others, some of whom carry weapons strapped to their backs, wear the knitted kipas and plaid shirts of the settlers. The women, who often outnumber the men, crowd into an area perhaps a third the size, although they are just as fervent in their petitions.

Had I come on another night, I might have caught the soldiers' ceremony, at which new recruits are presented with a Bible and a gun. But it is Friday, the beginning of Shabbat, and groups of young yeshiva students, many of them visiting Americans in search of spiritual enrichment and a possible mate, descend on the Wall. Arm in arm, dressed in their finest outfits, the students sing at the top of their lungs.

A half-hour later, I hear the Muslim call to prayer, followed by the peal of church bells. All of the songs are beautiful, and all are calling skyward. Each follows the score outlined by its respective composer, but someone has neglected to co-ordinate the symphonies.

"WHAT IS JERUSALEM?" ASKS ALLISON HODGKINS, an American academic who writes about Israeli settlement policy in East Jerusalem. "The question might as well be who is God, or what is faith? Jerusalem is, in the words of an Armenian Jerusalemite, a city of mirrors, where each person's vision of the city depends on the angle from which they look through the glass."

I stroll through the crowded Muslim Quarter, the highest-density neighbourhood in Israel, passing a Jewish yeshiva. Though non-Jews are not permitted to buy property in the Jewish Quarter, Jews may move into the Muslim Quarter. Local Arabs resent the incursions as an attempt to displace them, which settlers admit is the eventual goal. An enormous banner of the Star of David, unfurled from a yeshiva window, is marred by a splash of red paint, bright as blood.

I stop into Love Cassette, a gift shop that houses what must be the world's remaining supply of Garfield memorabilia. The owner, Tariq, is a good-looking young Palestinian born in Jerusalem.

"What do you think of Israel?" he asks. "Good or bad?"

Black and white questions are not my strong point. I hedge.

"I think bad," he says, answering his own question. He says he was studying in Germany until September 11, when his worried parents insisted he return. Soon after, Israeli police arrested him on suspicion of rock-throwing. He spent a week in prison. He says, indignantly, that he was out of the country when the alleged incident took place. "I tell them, what do you think, I throw rocks from Germany?"

In the crowded Arab market outside Damascus Gate I meet Hassan, a cheerful, muscular electronics vendor. I sit under his bright-coloured umbrella, and he teaches me the tricks of his trade. He calls the women "my sister" and exchanges returned merchandise with no questions asked. Like the other vendors, he doesn't issue receipts—he keeps a mental record of all his customers. He says the little boys are "very thieves," requiring him to have eyes in his stomach. He shoos them away when they gather, like young hyenas, around his CD players and TV sets. "*Yalla!*" he shouts. "Get going!" He tells me about the woman who sent her daughter to "talk sexy" to him while she slipped things into her bag.

As crowds of Arab shoppers mill about, buying socks from the sock vendor, alarm clocks from the alarm clock vendor, bread and herbs and olives, Hassan points out various people and gives me the inside story. He tells me which boy is honest, which man likes to flirt with other women despite having a very nice wife and a new daughter, which teenaged boy is doing cocaine. He tells me he is a very good snooker player and has been teaching a nineteen-year-old boy in Bethlehem, where he lives, how to play. Last night he saw the boy's name on television. Dead, shot in the chest by an Israeli bullet while watching TV with his family in their living room.

"This is war," Hassan says. "This is exactly war."

There have been many civilian deaths in Bethlehem in recent days. Hassan got a late start this morning because it took him four hours to drive a distance that, by direct roads, should take twenty minutes. He buys all his goods in Tel Aviv—though I wonder how—and keeps the receipts in his shirt pocket in case he is stopped and questioned.

I ask him if he is afraid, and he says, no, this is normal. But it is impossible to sleep at night with all the gunfire. I ask him if he thinks there will ever be peace. He says, never. Never peace. This has been going on since Mohammad, since Moses. "But we hope," he says.

He sends a boy to bring us tea with mint. I sit listening to a vendor who has laid his hands on a loudspeaker and is shouting, to the chagrin of all who must listen, that he is selling his goods at cost. "Liar," says Hassan, with a wink.

Hassan used to be a professional lute player. He would entertain at parties. Now, he says, there are no more parties. For ten years he played for a radio station in Tel Aviv. The Israeli musicians he performed with, he says, "they are still my best friends." But he has to feel quiet in order to play. It has been a long time since he has felt quiet.

I ask if the situation makes him sad.

"Of course it makes me sad. It makes the Jewish people sad also, when their people die. Most people here, the small people, they want peace. Just to live."

His friend Amir joins us. Amir wears a madras shirt. From one sleeve protrudes a withered hand. Amir has four children, ages one to eight. He tells me about them. The oldest wants to be a doctor. Amir is pleased about this. His son must become a doctor. The next, a girl, wishes to become a teacher. The five-year-old boy wants to be a soldier. The one-year-old, he isn't sure yet.

Soldiers have a way of getting killed, I remind him.

Amir says he doesn't want his son to learn to kill. "He will defend our homeland."

Hassan's friend won't believe me when I tell him there are Jewish Israelis who want to make peace with Palestinians. "They want us out," he insists. "They want our land. They want us to go to Syria or Jordan or Egypt." It is true that Rehavam Ze'evi, the Israeli tourism minister who was recently gunned down, had openly espoused the idea of "transfer," as does his replacement. A special kind of tour for the Arab population, one might say.

Amir pulls out his wallet. He shows me a photo of his ten-year-old nephew, killed seven months earlier by a bullet to the head. "On tv, the Jewish say they want peace, they want peace. And when we turn around, they shoot us in the back."

Does he think there will ever be peace? "Someday, God willing. In Jerusalem there are three peoples, Muslim, Jew and Christian. Why can't we live together? Why not?"

cnn interviewed him last week, Amir says. They wanted to know if there was freedom for Palestinians, or "unfreedom."

"And what did you tell them?"

"Unfreedom."

Later, I buy a compilation of Arabic pop songs from a cramped, hole-in-the-wall cd store. A Palestinian girl in a tight, rainbow-striped T-shirt selects a cd of British house music. Around a corner, in front of some deserted souvenir shops, I come upon a group of young men, Palestinian Jerusalemites, playing a game of cards. An ornate bronze platter serves as their card table. They invite me to sit down and play. Two young ultra-Orthodox stroll past, their ear locks blowing gently in the breeze. Shouldn't Jews be afraid to wander through Arab areas? I ask the card players.

"No," says one of them, looking surprised. "In Jerusalem, we have peace."

They try to teach me the game. It is five games in one, they explain.

As soon as I think I have the hang of it, the game changes.

"It's complicated," I say.

Yes, they nod.

"Like life," I say.

They nod. They appreciate this.

"Like Jerusalem," I say, enhancing my entertainment value.

They like this even more.

In *Jerusalem, City of Mirrors,* the Israeli author Amos Elon writes, "Card games make irresistible metaphors for writers on Jerusalem." He goes on to quote the Jerusalem poet Dennis Silk: "Whoever shuffled Jerusalem had a wicked pack of cards; a good many hands have been dealt and the vicious game goes on."

I get up to leave. The game goes on without me.

CHAPTER 5

The Middle Ground

Palestinian children, Hebron

ABOVE JERUSALEM, Apache helicopters hover in the night sky. The air vibrates with their ominous drone. In the distance, a peal like thunder.

"Rain?" I ask a Palestinian vendor.

"Tanks," he answers.

Not here, in the city of peace. Out there, minutes away, the widening war is being waged. Strains of intifada songs carry through the littered streets of Arab East Jerusalem. In the window of a Palestinian taxi, a banner: "To Be Free One Day." In the window of another: "Live Free or Die."

The next morning I hire a taxi from Damascus Gate to Hebron, a thirty-kilometre journey south of Jerusalem. My driver, Nassem, is a good-natured Palestinian Jerusalemite whose van has Israeli licence plates. At twenty-two, he is an old hand at ferrying journalists and news crews into the West Bank.

We take the Tunnel Road, a heavily fortified route opened five years ago to connect Israeli settlements in the West Bank while bypassing dense Palestinian areas such as Bethlehem and Deheishe refugee camp. The smoothly paved bypass roads are off-limits to vehicles with Palestinian plates, though a few Palestinians make their way along them riding donkeys. Above us looms the Arab village of Beit Jala. Opposite Beit Jala is Gilo, a Jewish settlement built on Beit Jala's orchards.

High cement barricades line the road to shield drivers, mainly settlers and army personnel, from gunfire. Palestinian gunmen fire on Gilo from Beit Jala, shooting from the outskirts of the village or from the forcibly commandeered houses of Beit Jala's terrified residents. The Israeli army and air force respond by shelling Beit Jala, driving more of its residents from their homes. Today, Gilo looks as serene as any well-planned condo complex. In Beit Jala, the houses facing the settlement have enormous chunks of mortar missing; their window frames are charred like blackened eyes. Some of the people I will meet in Hebron have lived briefly in these ravaged homes to try to limit the fighting. They have been described as "human shields," though they don't like to use the term.

Nassem stops at the first checkpoint. Two Israeli soldiers with M-16s pull open the side door of the van and crane their necks inside, checking that no one is stowed away in the back. Since 1993, the Israeli military has required Palestinians to apply for permits to travel into East Jerusalem or through Israel between the West Bank and Gaza. These soldiers glance over Nassem's ID and my passport, then wave us on.

We pass through a second and a third checkpoint without event. Bored soldiers lean on posts piled with food and cigarette packs, dreaming of their next leave, their girlfriends. Israeli tanks are parked at the entrance to some Arab villages; next to one an Israeli flag is strung from the ruins of a stone building. The slogan "No Arabs, no terrorist attacks" is scrawled in Hebrew on barriers, bus stops and boulders. Gated settlement follows gated settlement. Armed settlers in baseball caps and knitted kipas congregate near the front gates of one. In their Bermuda shorts and baggy T-shirts, they look American. Many are, Nassem tells me.

All around us, the landscape is rocky, arid, marked with grapevines and stubby trees. It is hard to believe that so many are willing to fight and even die for this land.

A hill of rubble blocks the turnoff for Hebron, part of the "closure" policy designed to restrict Palestinian movement. Nassem ably manoeuvres the van over a section flattened by other intrepid drivers. "Getting through is a matter of luck," he says. "If you have luck or not." Today we have luck. But once the army discovers this "around-way," as Palestinians call these breaks in the siege, they will block it off again.

In the mid-1990s, under the Oslo framework, control of the West Bank and Gaza was divided into Areas A, B and C. Area C, under Israeli military control and including all of the settlements, makes up 59 per cent of the occupied territories. Area B, a further 24 per cent, is under joint Israeli/Palestinian control: the Palestinian Authority (PA) oversees civil matters such as utilities, and the Israeli military handles security. Area A, under PA administration, makes up the remaining 17 per cent. It is here that the larger Palestinian population centres are located. Since the Israeli army controls the bypass roads that divide these non-contiguous regions (often referred to as Bantustans, after the black "homelands" established in apartheid South Africa), the army also decides who comes and goes.

In the space of five minutes, Nassem and I travel from an Israeli-controlled area to a Palestinian-controlled area to an Israeli-controlled area again. Skirmishes are concentrated on the borders. Crossing points are marked by signs of fighting—blackened cement blocks, rubble, garbage.

In a town in Area A, a ramshackle checkpoint flies a Palestinian flag, but no one is on duty. "They are afraid of Jewish soldiers," Nassem says.

The stores sell carpets, furnishings, foodstuffs. Every spare section of wall space is covered in Arabic graffiti, spray-painted in the colours of the Palestinian flag. Nassem translates a message signed by a Palestinian militant group: "Continue the intifada and make it more painful for the Jewish side and more good for us."

Nassem leaves me at the drop-off point in Hebron 1, the Palestinian-controlled sector of the divided city. He makes me promise to phone him if I run into trouble.

I WAIT ON THE CORNER of a busy intersection. Taxis ease in and out of a massive traffic snarl. A smiling man wades into the fray with a tin barrel strapped to his chest and a siphon in one hand, selling coffee car to car. Across the street is a bustling market. Stands are set up under wide umbrellas, selling produce, spices and cheap sundry items from hair barrettes to underwear. At one clothing stand, sexy silver chain-mail tank tops glitter and sway in the warm breeze. If any of the women flooding past are buying such wares, they are concealing them well under long dark robes.

I am here to interview members of the Christian Peacemaker Team, or CPT, a Mennonite-based organization of North American volunteers who believe that if others are willing to risk their lives for war, they as pacifists should take some risks for peace. Committed to reducing violence by "Getting in the Way," the "CPTers" serve in hot spots such as Colombia, Chiapas, Afghanistan and here in Hebron.

Greg Rollins comes to meet me. The amiable twenty-eight-year-old from British Columbia wears a white cotton shirt, khakis and a red CPT baseball cap over his crewcut hair. He is so low-key I wonder if he knows where he is, though such a temperament is surely an asset when you have to sleep through nightly gunfire and early-morning Muslim calls to prayer. I soon discover that his calm exterior hides a wry sense of humour. When I ask him why he has come to Hebron, he says, with a deadpan expression, "To avoid child support payments."

We wend our way past the market, toward the littered, sand-spattered streets that separate H-1 from H-2. The streets call to mind the words of William Zinsser, who wrote about the sand streets of Timbuktu. "Every town starts with dirt streets that eventually get paved as the inhabitants prosper. But sand represents defeat. A city with streets of sand is a city at the edge."

Hebron is such a city. Under the terms of the 1997 Israeli-Palestinian Interim Agreement, Hebron received special status due to the presence of Israeli settlements in the heart of the city. The city was sectioned into two parts: H-1, some 80 per cent of Hebron, under Palestinian Authority jurisdiction (Area A); and H-2, containing the Old City of Hebron and the settlers, under Israeli military control (Area B) but for municipal matters.

As Rollins explains, the 30,000 Palestinian inhabitants of H-2 live alongside 500 of the most militant Jewish settlers on the West Bank (known among soldiers as the "settlers' mafia") and the 2,500 soldiers and police who are assigned to protect them. At the border between H-1 and H-2, Palestinian gunmen and Israeli security forces collide. The metal doors on the market stalls are pockmarked by bullet holes. Fire has blackened cement barriers. Some buildings lie in ruins. Across the street, the first floor of a building is burned out; on the second floor a man lounges on his balcony, enjoying the sun and a cigarette as if he's on the Riviera.

Compared to the flourishing market and crowds of H-1, H-2 is a wasteland. It is only ten in the morning, but most of the shops lining the kasbah have already locked up. A few older men in long robes and white kaffiyehs still sit outside talking or smoking, but most people have returned to their homes. Greg says soldiers went through an hour before my arrival and ordered everyone to close up. Tonight is the start of Yom Kippur, the holiest day in the Jewish calendar, and the local settlers have guests.

Curfews like these are the equivalent of around-the-clock house arrest; they can last longer than a week at a stretch. A UN report notes that in the nine months following September 2000, the Palestinians in H-2 were under curfew for all or part of 130 days. Under curfew, residents (with the exception of the settlers, to whom curfews do not apply) must stay inside their homes. At the moment, a special agreement allows schoolchildren and teachers to attend school. If the curfew runs longer than four or five days, soldiers let the residents out for a few hours to buy food.

On certain days, under curfew, the skies above Hebron fill with kites. Local children, confined to their homes, go onto their rooftops to fly the contraptions they have made from sticks, string and plastic garbage bags. Curfews frighten the children, but the act of flying kites soothes their fears. When the wind is right, the kites hover above the city for hours.

Rolls of barbed wire sit like errant tumbleweeds beside the CPT apartment building. A few weeks ago, Israeli soldiers strung it across the entranceway and deemed the building a closed military zone. The team tried to extract an explanation from the army, but no one could provide them with a straight answer. Under threat of arrest, the CPTers defied the order and went inside. Soon after, the order was lifted. The barbed wire remains, pushed off to the side.

Their main apartment is about as basic as it gets. A squat toilet is flushed with a jug of dirty water from a barrel. Two rooms with cots and mattresses on the floor serve as sleeping quarters. In the office, outfitted with two laptops from which they email their reports, is a well-stocked bookcase containing works by Amos Oz, Margaret Atwood, Hanan Ashrawi, Charles Dickens, Don DeLillo, Simon Wiesenthal and Gandhi. *Memoirs of a Geisha* sits not far from half a shelf of Bibles and two copies of the Koran, though Greg says he's fine as long as he has *The Lord of the Rings.*

Sitting on a donated couch, we are joined by George Weber, a retired history teacher from Ontario. He has a kindly face and a grandfatherly demeanour. One of the *Let's Go* guidebooks suggests stopping by Hebron to meet the "mild-mannered CPTers." It's hard to think of a more apt description of these two.

George first travelled to the region as a backpacker in 1947. That year, prior to the creation of the modern state of Israel, he met Palestinian refugees in Jordan and later spent a week on a kibbutz. He had a chance to hear both sides of the story. "The sad thing," he says, "is not all that much has really changed."

The door opens and a man with long shaggy hair enters, carrying a box of baklava. A first-year anthropology student from Cambridge University, Mika Minao dropped by Hebron to volunteer during his summer vacation.

"Did you notice the settlers have a lot of visitors?" says Mika, passing around the box of honeyed sweets.

"For the holidays," says Greg.

"They were coming around and taking pictures of the market," Mika says.

"I'm sure they were," says Greg.

By law, Israelis are prohibited from setting foot in Area A, such as the local market in H-1. But Greg says that the settlers sometimes, for whatever reason, go in and knock over a few of the Palestinian market stalls. The soldiers, fearing a Palestinian reprisal, respond by imposing a curfew on the Palestinian population.

So what exactly does the team do here?

"We're like firemen," says George.

Most days, they wait for an emergency call. Like yesterday, when George and Mika were called to escort children to school. Most of the children had made it through the Israeli checkpoint. (Checkpoints are scattered throughout Hebron to monitor the streets Palestinians and settlers jointly use, or set up at random locations, for hours at a time, where soldiers decide whether Palestinian residents will be turned back, detained, arrested or granted passage.) "Then," says George, "the soldier in charge decided no more." A soldier pointed his gun at one little girl and told her to move back; her mother, determined the girl would make it to school, ordered her to stay put. Eventually, all of the children were permitted to go to school.

George says most of the soldiers don't want to harm anyone. "They're here to keep the peace. But there are individuals who are very aggressive. They give the impression they wouldn't mind shooting somebody."

That same day George went to see about a break-in at a local Palestinian shop. A group of settlers and their children were harassing the shopkeeper, and the settler children hurled stones at George. Soldiers were present but did not intervene.

"Soldiers are just kids with guns," says Greg. "If I was eighteen and given a gun, I'd let the power go to my head." It's difficult to picture Greg drunk with power, but given the right set of circumstances, I suppose it could happen.

The team has its own weaponry: often the presence of their cameras is all it takes to diffuse a situation. "They don't want another picture like the one that was shown," says George, referring to twelve-year-old Mohammad al-Durrah, the Palestinian boy shot in his father's arms in Gaza, the incident caught on film and broadcast around the world.

Their other weapon is a cell phone. When a Palestinian is shot, the families often summon the CPTers or ask them to contact police, who tend to respond more expediently when internationals make the call.

Last week, the CPTers were called after two civilians were killed in the fighting. When they arrived at the scene, the victims had already been taken away by ambulance, but people were still covered in blood, and one man, a cousin to the victims, had passed out from the shock. The area was under curfew. Soldiers, themselves highly stressed, were trying to get people to return to their homes, but no one was listening. In a case such as this, the CPT presence may have helped prevent an escalation.

Other times, the team visits the sites of house demolitions. Israelis claim the homes were built without proper permits, whereas Palestinians claim such permits are impossible to acquire. The CPTers also document settlement expansion. "The settlers take out the fence and move it twenty-five or however many metres and say this is now Jewish land," Greg explains.

Lately, he adds, "There have been a lot of stories here about soldiers entering people's homes and saying they are searching for weapons and trashing the place, destroying things, then leaving. Or they'll take one of the men and detain him." Under Israeli military law, Palestinians in the West Bank and Gaza can be imprisoned for up to six months without learning the charges or going before a judge, after which time their "administrative detention" can be renewed.

The problem, as George sees it, is that Israelis have become "hostage to a minority"—the settlers—"who believe that this is Jewish soil." He thinks the Israeli government is complicit, and the American government is acquiescent. "But in a war situation, you're either for or against, and that's the difficulty. The middle ground becomes untenable."

On the table is a bowl of grapes, a gift from local Palestinians to thank the CPTers for watching that the settlers don't shoot them while they harvest. Mika hands me instead a bowl of bullet casings, and another filled with spent tear-gas canisters, concussion grenades, flares and rubber bullets that the CPTers have collected around town. On one of the grenades is written, "The federal laboratories will not be responsible for the misuse . . ."

"People have said to me that this is their worst year since 1967," says Mika. "But it's encouraging to see the endurance people have. Obviously people start to hate the system, but many say they don't hate Jews, they hate the system, and they're against the suicide bombers."

"They don't hate American people, American culture," adds George. "They hate American policy, Israeli policy." And the American military hardware that is being used against them.

The results of the team's work can seem feeble in the face of such an intransigent conflict. One woman on their team, returning after a year abroad, was shocked to find that many more streets are now closed to Palestinians, that fewer shops are reopening after curfews are lifted. George says you can't look at it that way. "You have to think, if you can help the headmaster of a school to get his students to class one day, that's a small victory."

We have been joined by Anne Montgomery, one of the team leaders. At seventy-four, she is as lean as a marathon runner; she wears her cropped white hair brushed forward. She is a New Yorker, a Roman Catholic nun and a dedicated peace activist who has done time in the American prison system for breaking into a nuclear installation and damaging a warhead. She also spent six weeks living in Beit Jala as part of her activism, some of the time in a room facing the settlement of Gilo.

One day, sitting in the room, she heard machine-gun fire outside the window and took refuge in the bathroom. When she emerged, a hole from a 50-millimetre shell had punctured the wall where her head had been. "People who live there say it was never shelled before the CPTers got there," she says. "All the army has to do is enclose the villages and the people starve. It was a relief to come back to Hebron after Beit Jala." Anne has lived in Hebron on and off for six years. She has witnessed the situation deteriorate in that time. "I am bitter and cynical," she tells me. Even so, she keeps coming back here, keeps working for peace.

Non-violence is at the core of the CPT mission. The army knows how to deal with force, they say, but non-violent resistance confuses them. Not long ago, Greg joined a group of Palestinian and Israeli activists who were removing roadblocks near the West Bank town of Nablus. The army ordered them to stop and arrested those who refused.

"First," says Greg, "they wanted us to sign statements saying we wouldn't come back to the area for two months, and we refused. Then they wanted us to sign statements saying we could come back whenever we wanted but we had to pay a 3,000-shekel fine, and we refused. Then they said we didn't have to pay a 3,000-shekel fine, we could come back to the area whenever we wanted, but we had to show up in court in two weeks, and if we didn't show up in court we would have to pay a 5,000-shekel fine, and we refused. Then they said, Okay, you can all leave but [well-known Israeli peace activist] Neta Golan cannot leave, and we refused. And then they said, Okay. Get out. Here's your passports. Get out. By the way, please sign this before you leave. And we refused."

How do the CPTers reconcile their position with obeying the law?

"As far as we're concerned, closing off our apartment and calling it a closed military zone is harassment," Greg says. "It's not the law. If they are harassing a Palestinian or destroying a Palestinian's home, it may be the law, but it's a terrible law. So this is a way of bringing attention to unjust laws."

FROM THE ROOFTOP OF THE CPT RESIDENCE, the city looks calm and picturesque. In the distance, a Palestinian funeral procession follows the familiar path to a nearby cemetery. Directly below is a *hammam,* a Middle Eastern bathhouse that, like so many things, is no longer in use.

The team has a rule that members are not allowed on the roof during shooting. Once, on a day when shooting started early, a bullet whizzed past a member's head, so close he could feel the breeze. On at least two occasions, bullets have been fired into the CPT women's apartment, a floor up from the main residence, from the direction of the nearby settlement—once, while one of the women was inside. Settlers have punched the CPTers, kicked them, thrown stones, eggs, garbage. "They quite often call us 'Nazi' and spit at us," Greg shrugs, almost indifferently. Settlers are known to attack soldiers as well.

Greg and I take a walk through the Old City. The shops are closed, the streets empty. In the desolate marketplace are the ruins of ancient market stalls. A group of Israeli soldiers in full combat gear emerge into the sunlight from a dark alleyway and walk across our path, seemingly oblivious to our presence.

Two Palestinian women in long robes, their hair covered, walk toward us. One of them, young and pretty, stops and turns to Greg. She says something in Arabic and smiles shyly. Then, in careful English: "You . . . are . . . nice."

"*Shukran,*" says Greg. "Thank you." And smiles shyly in return.

We go to turn down a side street, but a soldier stops us.

"It is forbidden," the soldier says.

"Why?" Greg asks.

"It's forbidden."

"We need to go down there. We live down there. "

"No, you can't go."

"We have to go through there."

"It's forbidden."

"Why?"

The stand-off continues until the soldier gives up in frustration. I have learned my first lesson in non-violent resistance. It involves wearing the other guy down.

We walk down the forbidden street. In front of a small house, a group of children are playing. A boy of about five runs over and holds up his fingers in the V-sign, then stands there so I can take his photograph. I think at first that his hand signal means peace, or maybe victory, but Greg says no, he thinks that here it means something else. Here, he thinks, it means freedom.

Greg doesn't take all tales of woe at face value. A kid will approach him with a scratch on his face and tell him a soldier did it, when Greg knows he probably fell off his bicycle. The truth is war's first casualty. It's important to watch closely and think for yourself.

Greg points out the Tomb of the Patriarchs across the street, where settler Baruch Goldstein shot and killed twenty-nine Arabs during prayers and wounded a hundred more in 1994. Dr. Goldstein, originally from Brooklyn, was an advocate of "transfer," the policy of expelling, by force if necessary, the Palestinian population to the Arab states (a strategy supported by 46 per cent of Jewish Israelis, according to Tel Aviv University's Jaffee Center for Strategic Studies, the flip side of the 49 per cent who advocate dismantling most of the settlements and leaving the occupied territories in exchange for a peace agreement). Today, Goldstein's gravesite is a pilgrimage for far-right Israelis.

A youth, pale and freckled, approaches and urges us to come into his house. We follow him inside. He shows us—the locks have been smashed off all the doors. It happened that morning. The soldiers told him they were looking for guns, he says. The youth's mother, small and frail, wearing a long white hijab over her hair, stands in the shadows, clasping and unclasping her hands.

I don't have any gun, the youth tells me in Hebrew. He asked the soldiers to wait for someone to bring the keys. Just five minutes, someone would bring them the keys. When he talks, his face contorts; one side moves but the other seems frozen.

Every room in the house has been ransacked. What belongings the family has, mostly clothing, are lying in heaps on the floor. The couches and chairs have been turned over and slashed open, front and back.

In the upstairs room, the mattress—there is no bed—is ripped open, the stuffing torn out. A TV set lies gutted on the floor.

The youth is saying he has to stay inside during the curfew, he cannot go to work, and now he has no TV to pass the days and no money to buy another. "Every two weeks the soldiers come," he says. "They say if we sell our house to the Jews, no more problems."

The house smells of sweat and fear. The mother remains in the shadows. All she can do is look at me, and clasp and unclasp her hands.

I listen for as long as I can stand it, then we go. Greg says that before the soldiers started looking for guns, they would enter Palestinian homes and take photographs, then bring out tape measures and measure all the rooms. No one knew what they were doing, but it gave Greg an idea. "When I'm in charge, I'm going to have an Interior Decorating Army." He brightens. "A lot of things will change when I'm in charge."

A WEEK LATER, AT A FASHIONABLE wine bar near the Tel Aviv stock exchange—voices careening off the ceiling, abstract paintings high upon the walls—I am sitting at a long bar surrounded by young Israelis who all wear fashionable black or white. Two of them ask me: "So what is your opinion of the matter? Tell us. Don't hold back."

The young people drink German beer and smoke Marlboro cigarettes or long slim Capris. At nearby tables, cutlery tinkles as black-clad waitresses swoop in with steaming plates as artful as the canvases.

I think of the young woman in Hebron, also wearing black with a white headscarf, smiling shyly at the young man who had come, in his small way, to make things better. Failing that, to observe for himself the way life is. To bear witness.

I tell them what I've seen, and after I speak they ask me if the house that was raided did not actually harbour guns. If perhaps the soldiers weren't correct to raid it. If they weren't measuring the houses to see if there were secret hiding places where guns could be stored. Of course, I say. All of this is possible.

The music ricochets off the ceiling and I order another glass of Israeli Riesling, which has a sweet tang I like, and later we pass through to the courtyard where tables are set up under trees. People are considering their options for nocturnal adventure and wondering how they will ever be able to get up for work in the morning. And I think: they are free to get up and go to work in the morning. They live with fear, but it does not, without reprisal, enter their homes at an unknown hour. I think of the mother, clasping and unclasping her hands, who knows there will be other days like this one, other raids; who watches the rage of her son, yet is helpless to stem the tide of despair that threatens to flood her town and carry all of them away. Clasped or unclasped, there is nothing for her hands to grasp.

CHAPTER 6

The End of Utopia

Groomed pathway, Kibbutz Ma'agan Mikhael

*T*HE BUS DRIVER has a genius for finding Phil Collins, wherever Phil may be lurking on the radio, and singing along in a thick Hebrew accent. The space around his seat is strung with stuffed animals such as Tweety Pie and "soccer-ball man," as well as a soccer team pennant for Hapoel Tel Aviv and both an Israeli and an American flag.

He drops me off outside Kibbutz Ma'agan Mikhael, an hour up the coast from Tel Aviv. I hitchhike the few kilometres from the main road, past swaying banana groves, into the kibbutz. It is an idyllic place, land-scaped to Club Med standards. One of Israel's foremost cactus experts lives here, and the startling cactus gardens attract visitors from around the country.

I wait outside the *cheder ochel,* the "food room" where the entire community gathers to chow down cafeteria-style. The kibbutz reminds me of an upscale summer camp. People of all ages come and go along groomed pathways, most riding bikes that nobody bothers to lock up, some looking grubbed-out from a workday that starts early. Many of the bicycles sport left-wing bumper stickers and the plastic baskets the kibbutz manufactures. Some older kibbutz members whiz around in motorized carts.

Since everyone knows everyone on a kibbutz, I have already fielded a few quizzical glances by the time Mike Schlesinger arrives to greet me. Trim and fit-looking, wearing a faded polo shirt and Bermuda shorts, Mike appears younger than his fifty-something years. His friendly, open face exudes a relaxed confidence that is distinctly American. He and his wife, Lauri, made aliyah (from the Hebrew for "ascent") from Los Angeles to Israel in the early 1970s. It was at the height of an idealistic North American immigration that reached a peak of more than 8,000 in 1971, propelled by the heady optimism that followed the triumphs of the 1967 Six-Day War. Today's North American immigrants are far fewer— only about 1,500 a year. Unlike the Schlesingers, who are devoutly secular, these new Israelis tend to be religious, often moving to settlements in the occupied territories.

Mike and Lauri have been living on Kibbutz Ma'agan Mikhael for twenty years. This is where they've raised their four children, aged fourteen to twenty-eight. So far, all of the kids are still living on the kibbutz, though they have yet to decide if they want to become members. In most kibbutzim, the younger generation is moving away en masse.

Mike ushers me into the crowded dining hall. Near the entryway are two computers where kibbutz members sign out the communal cars, a luxury they pay for out of their personal allowance money. We grab a tray and join the noisy queue, where my plate is slopped with processed

corn sticks (though I also have a choice of fish or turkey), some uniden-
tifiable noodle concoction, sweet beets and overcooked carrots. Not
great, but substantial. And as Mike reminds me several times, I am welcome to seconds, even thirds.

Mike opts for the turkey and a mug of grape Kool-Aid. We find a
table near the window, where the five-star view of the Mediterranean
almost makes up for what the cuisine is lacking. Around us, the sounds
of hundreds of forks striking hundreds of plates, animated conversation, laughter.

Ma'agan Mikhael, established a half-century ago, is one of the few
kibbutzim where everyone still eats together and pools money and
resources. Other than the clothes on people's backs, almost everything
is communally owned. They still follow a "from each according to his
abilities, to each according to his needs" philosophy, an example of a
decentralized, democratic communism that actually works.

Well, worked.

"This is what all the kibbutzim used to be like," says Mike. "Now
we're the exception to the rule, because most kibbutzim are in a period
of very, very drastic change—the economic system is changing, the
social system is changing, very, very drastically. So if you come back in
a few years there may not be anything you'd recognize as a kibbutz any
more."

The kibbutzim, once the lifeblood of the fledgling nation, are part of
what inspired my original interest in Israel. I was enamoured of the
images of self-sacrificing pioneers who devoted their lives to planting
gardens in the desert—gardens a lot like the ones I see here—and of
people who placed national service ahead of personal gain.

Today's kibbutz members are still serving their nation. In *The
Kibbutz: Awakening from Utopia,* Daniel Gavron writes that, while com-
prising "less than 3 percent of the population, the kibbutzim still grow
and raise 40 percent of the country's agricultural produce, make 10 percent of its industrial output, and produce 7 percent of its exports. Half

the volunteers in the army's elite combat units and nearly a third of its air force pilots are children of the kibbutz. Almost a fifth of the army's young officers are kibbutzniks."

But the majority view is that the movement born at the outset of the twentieth century as a synthesis of Zionism and socialism is in its final days. Due to financial problems brought on by crumbling agricultural prices and plain old fiscal mismanagement, most kibbutzim are scrambling to find their way out of a dark pit. Many of the problems surfaced in the mid-1980s, when the government took steps to curb hyperinflation that had spiked as high as 400 per cent. The money kibbutzim had been borrowing abruptly caught up with them. Today, their combined debt lies in the billions of dollars.

Most of the some 265 remaining kibbutzim are privatizing and rethinking their socialist ways. People aren't so sure they want 80 or 90 per cent of their income going into a communal pot. Maybe they don't use the community sports hall or like the movies at the community theatre; maybe they would prefer to cook their own meals at home. "The changes," as they are known in kibbutz parlance, have been radical. Three-fourths of kibbutzim now charge members for meals. Some kibbutzim make ends meet by renting out their facilities for wedding receptions. Others are hanging on in hopes the government will allow them to sell their publicly owned land, turning them into instant millionaires. Even on this relatively traditional kibbutz, the dirty word "self-fulfillment" is being bandied about in polite company. Whereas jobs used to be assigned by the kibbutz, many people now want the freedom to choose career paths that better align with their interests and abilities. Some members of Ma'agan Mikhael find employment outside the kibbutz, though their salaries still return to the community.

Values too have shifted. Not only on the kibbutzim, but everywhere; not only in Israel, but around the world. People want to keep more of what they earn. They want more choice about where that money goes. And then there are the shopping malls.

"That kind of consumerism is really an incredibly gigantic change," says Mike, between bites. "Gigantic change. When we came to the country, there wasn't such a thing as a shopping mall. There was no such thing. It did *not* exist. There were little tiny hole-in-the-wall stores and a Middle Eastern souk in a lot of cities and consumerism was not an issue. You went into a store and there were two kinds of toothpaste, that was it."

There was no McDonald's, no Office Depot, no Best Buy, no Starbucks. There was no cable—just a communal television and a scant few channels. And that was how Mike and Lauri liked it.

"Going into a store and having to choose between two kinds of toothpaste was for me exactly where I wanted to be," Mike says. "And now Israel represents almost America on a smaller scale."

Still, Mike thinks he and Lauri would make the same decision if they had it to do all over again. Even with the growing consumerism, even with the constant crises, even though it causes both parents great anxiety to have their children serve in the army. Mike himself did four months of army training at the age of thirty and served in the reserves for years afterward, including a stint in the Lebanon War.

"If you take the modern history, from '48 to today, it's one long war," he says. "This is the same war."

Is there still that fear of annihilation?

"Yes. I'd say it's palpable. And it's not some kind of neurosis or something. The country's been through wars constantly."

Mike's daughter approaches our table. She is a lovely young woman of twenty, a vision of health. Today was her final day of army service.

I congratulate her. "Are you happy?" I ask.

"Very," she beams, before leaving to join her friends.

Mike explains that the kibbutz sponsors its members' children through a university degree, so long as the children work for a year on the kibbutz following their army service. His daughter will spend this year working. His two older sons, like many of their peers, postponed university to spend several years travelling after their army service. Like many of their peers, they returned with questions about life in Israel.

"They came back thinking this is not a normal society. Maybe it would be a lot nicer not to have to live like this. Maybe it would be a lot more pleasant to live in Norway or Denmark." Mike pauses. "And you know what? They're right. Of course they're right. There would be about a thousand places that would be more comfortable—I wouldn't use the word normal, but less stressful, less dangerous, where you have much less commitment other than paying your taxes. Where else in the world do you have to serve in the reserves up to the age of forty-five? And put your life on the line—not just go to some place and play games for a couple weeks—but put your life on the line? Where do you have to do that?"

We load our dishes onto the line of dish racks that move along a conveyor belt. I shudder at the thought of being assigned kitchen duty for the kibbutz's 1,500 residents. Despite an egalitarian ethos, at most kibbutzim women are still predominant in kitchen, laundry and child care services.

Leaving the dining hall, we head downstairs to the two movie theatres, where *Toy Story* has been playing for a group of children. We walk past the art display and out onto palm-tree–lined pathways, the heady scent of tropical flowers in the air, crushed petals under our feet. I comment on the beauty of the landscaping. Mike says the guy in charge is devoted to the task, but now people complain that the gardening wastes too much water.

"You can't win," he says.

And besides, the landscaping guy will be replaced soon. Leadership roles rotate every two years to prevent the development of a leadership class.

"It's a big, big problem," says Mike. Few people are willing and able to take positions of leadership, and there aren't any perks. "You don't get a bigger car, you don't get a bigger apartment, you don't get more money, you don't get more anything except more responsibility and more headaches and more criticism of you by everybody else."

We pass the coffee house, where two women are huddled close together, talking. They fall silent the moment they see us approaching. Gossip is endemic on kibbutzim, worse than in small towns. We pass the grassy open area where the community gathers to celebrate the Jewish holidays in secular kibbutzim style. Some kibbutzim are so secular they serve pork.

"Did you fast for Yom Kippur?"

"No," says Mike. "I celebrated by taking the day off."

We return to our discussion of the growing number of Israelis who openly contemplate leaving Israel. Talk is a lot different from action, Mike points out. In the late sixties and early seventies, he and Lauri spent their summers leading teams of Jewish-American high-school students on trips to Israel. They had to explain the importance of Israel to the Jewish identity, and in the process, they convinced themselves. After the victories of 1967, young Israelis would often confront them on their visits. "Why don't you come here?" they would ask. But soon after he and Lauri arrived, Mike adds ruefully, Israelis started asking them a different question: "Why did you come here?"

Farther on, Mike points out the old *beit yeledim,* "children's houses," where kids used to sleep apart from their parents. When the family was living on a different kibbutz, Mike and Lauri's first two children slept in one from the age of six weeks. Even though four hours in the late afternoon and evening were "children's hours," designated exclusively as family time—far more than the average family unit spends together today— Lauri had difficulty accepting the sleeping arrangements, which all kibbutzim have since abandoned. Ma'agan Mikhael disbanded the children's houses in 1981. Now, some kibbutz members believe that the end of the children's houses signalled the beginning of the end for the movement.

Mike shows me inside the plastics factory where he spends forty-five hours of each week. It manufactures, among other things, a successful line of high-tech toilet flushers. The factory is the lifeline of the kibbutz, and the reason its members have attained such an enviable standard of living. Ma'agan Mikhael had the forethought to industrialize in the mid-1960s, at a time when many kibbutzim were still dependent on agriculture. That's why this kibbutz has remained financially solvent and has not been forced to make drastic changes, Mike says. Till now.

Even though there is no financial imperative, many at Ma'agan Mikhael are beginning to question whether change isn't inevitable, part of the mysterious forces reshaping the world. You can see it more clearly in kibbutzim that have already succumbed. At Glil Yam, a kibbutz in the centre of Hertzliya, the buildings and grounds look as if they belong to absentee owners. Roads and sidewalks are falling apart. At noon, the dining hall hosts a handful of residents. Those who remain seem more like renters looking around for better prospects.

We sit on a bench, watching white birds peck at the grass, cooled by the breeze off the sea. I ask Mike if he feels fulfilled in this life.

"Fulfilled?" It's not a question that crosses his mind very often. I can tell it's not a question he approves of in principle. But yes, he says, he thinks he's fulfilled. What would he be doing better in southern California?

The idea of serving a cause greater than oneself is a concept of life that reaches beyond the newly ascendant ideal in Israeli society: making a buck. But something about the kibbutz seems slightly out of synch, almost anachronistic. The mantle of nation-building has moved to other shoulders. Today, another breed of pioneering Israeli is heeding the call of that undeniable enticement—a cause: something to fight for, to die for. For some, even to kill for.

Those who consider themselves the new Israeli pioneers are the Jewish settlers who have moved to the West Bank and Gaza, Mike says: "It's been a cliché over the last ten or fifteen years that they're the ones who have stolen the aura that used to belong to the kibbutzniks." Already, the children of settlers (who, though often religious, do not shirk army service as the ultra-Orthodox do) make up a growing proportion of elite army units, just as kibbutzniks once did.

Yet many kibbutzniks, coming from the left of the political spectrum, see the settlers who claim the West Bank and Gaza for a Greater Israel as a negative force. "Yitzhak Rabin was assassinated because he was considered a traitor for being willing to give the Palestinians land where Jews have now settled," says Mike "There are people who believed, and believe today, that his assassination was justified."

The kibbutzniks, once held in such esteem, are losing influence at a time when their presence is most needed. As I leave Ma'agan Mikhael, hitching a ride out to the main road in one of the communal cars, it is with the knowledge that a proud chapter in the short history of modern Israel has all but ended.

CHAPTER 7

The New Revolutionaries

Political posters, Jerusalem

*T*HE BULLETPROOF windows on the bus to the West Bank settlement of Efrat are cloudy, like cataracts. Passengers don't bother looking out, but rather stare into the middle distance. Since the tops of the windows are not reinforced, people sit down in the aisle when the seats are full rather than risk standing. This is what happens when you live behind barricades.

From their dress, most of the passengers appear to be religious. Most of the women wear modest skirts, long-sleeved shirts and determinedly unattractive hats or hairnets; the men wear knitted kipas and fringed shirts. I fixate on the woman in the seat behind the driver. She is heavy-set and stern, her iron-grey hair partly covered by a scarlet triangle scarf. She calls to mind Madame Defarge, the French revolutionary of Dickens's *A Tale of Two Cities*. The settlers are Israel's new revolutionaries, and the famous opening sentence of Dickens's novel could be written today.

It is the best or the worst of times, depending how you view the occupation. For it is Israel's thirty-five-year occupation of the West Bank and Gaza that lies at the heart of the Israeli-Palestinian conflict. And it is the Jewish settlers, whose population has doubled in the past ten years—to 200,000 in the West Bank (which they refer to by the Biblical names Judea and Samaria) and Gaza, and a further 200,000 in East Jerusalem—who are shaping Israel's future with a tireless zeal not found among the soft Tel Avivians busy pursuing their creature comforts.

Through the front window, shielded by a wire grid, I see billboard upon billboard advertising attractive houses in the settlements. The houses have red roofs, the Israeli equivalent of the white picket fence. One billboard shows a man relaxing on a bench, gazing at his new view. Another shows two little girls whispering to one another. This is the perfect place to buy an affordably priced dream home, the billboards promise, to raise a family. Many people have bought this vision, and the more seductive visions that float here in the air.

The sign for Efrat is written in Arabic, Hebrew and English, but someone has painted over the Arabic. I leave the bus and walk past rows of small white houses, charming flower gardens, a quaint town centre and a medical clinic. Some 1,300 families live in this well-off Modern Orthodox settlement, which hopes eventually to house 4,000. More than a third of the residents are native English speakers, many of them immigrants from the United States.

The streets are quiet. My footsteps and the nearby knell of construction are the only intrusions upon the tranquillity. Everyone seems to be at work or school except for one woman who pushes a baby carriage down the deserted sidewalk. Efrat, with its swimming pool and tennis courts, would appear idyllic if not for the number of cars with bulletproof windows, thick and yellowed like the skin of a callus. I walk up a steep hill to Neveh Shmuel boys' school to meet Shlomo Riskin, chief rabbi of Efrat.

Rabbi Riskin is originally from New York, where he received a doctorate in philosophy from New York University and founded Manhattan's Lincoln Square Synagogue, and he still maintains a New Yorker's schedule. His energetic secretary tells me she has tried twice to reach me to cancel our meeting. But no matter. We will work something out. I can ride with Rabbi Riskin to his appointments in Jerusalem and talk to him along the way.

Parked behind the school is the Ford Excursion, a sports utility vehicle the size of a small tank with buttery leather seats. Rabbi Riskin's driver is a bearish ultra-Orthodox with a bushy black beard and a kipa. He looks intimidating, as if he needs nothing more than a sword swinging from his side and a few token scalps dangling from his belt to complete the effect. Pulling out of the lot, he tells me he was born in France; we converse in a pidgin blend of French and Hebrew. He shares this job with another driver, since the rabbi is so busy. Efrat, the driver tells me, is 99 per cent religious. He himself is from the nearby ultra-Orthodox settlement of Beitar.

But it's not just religion that is propelling the growth of more than 150 settlements in the West Bank and Gaza. The Fourth Geneva Convention of 1949, signed and ratified by Israel, states that countries may not acquire territory by war and prohibits occupying powers from moving citizens onto occupied land. Yet the settlements continue to be a priority for the Israeli government. An aerial survey conducted by Peace Now revealed that at least fifteen new settlements were established in the West Bank in the ten weeks after Prime Minister Ariel Sharon—who in 1998, as Israel's foreign minister, urged settlement leaders to "grab the hilltops"—took office in March of 2001. The strategy of land appropriation and settlement building is often referred to as "creating facts on the ground."

Israel subsidizes the settlements with hundreds of millions of dollars in housing benefits, bypass roads, agricultural and investment subsidies, free preschool education and half-price public transit. These incentives have led many secular families with no ideological agenda—such as new immigrants—to move to the settlements. A report in *Ha'aretz* notes that the average government investment per person within the occupied territories is nearly three times the amount spent on inhabitants within Israel, even before the ongoing costs of army and security forces to protect the settlements are factored in.

The driver parks in front of a modest red-roofed house. Rabbi Riskin, when he emerges, is a short, animated man with a round chipmunk face. He wears a well-cut grey suit with a natty blue-and-grey tie and a matching knitted kipa. He is clearly a talker. And he doesn't waste time. As soon as he settles into his seat, he begins making phone calls.

"I sent the fax," he is saying in a nasal New York twang. "He's giving five-hundred thousand."

On his lap is a printout of the day's agenda. When the phone cuts out due to bad reception, he tells me he has been awake since five. He has already taught one class and is heading to another. Then to an interview with Channel 7, a pirate radio station run by settlers. Then to a class for rabbinical students, followed by another class and another radio interview in the evening. The driver, whose name is David, has told me Riskin often works until past midnight.

Rabbi Riskin makes a quick call to his wife, Victoria, who has just arrived in the United States for a synagogue event. He will join her, but she had to go early to acclimatize. "I never get jet lag," Riskin explains. I am not surprised. He seems indefatigable.

We fly past a lineup of Palestinian taxis waiting at a checkpoint to enter the Arab village of El Khader. Efrat is built partly on land confiscated from El Khader. A group of Palestinians stand around listlessly near the soldiers manning the dusty checkpoint.

"It's a difficult country in the last ten years," Riskin is saying. "Nineteen eighty-seven was the first intifada, but it wasn't as violent. It was before Oslo, when we gave the Palestinians guns."

The vehicle in front of us is a military jeep. We slow for another checkpoint, but the soldier nods us on. The checkpoints are not meant for settlers.

Rabbi Riskin tells me he chooses to live here because he believes the Torah prescribes that all Jews live in Israel. But there is another reason why he, a successful New Yorker, moved to Efrat. A reason that may be more important, for he will repeat it later in the day: "I believe that in our generation, post-Holocaust, whatever happens in the Diaspora is a footnote to Jewish history, and what happens in Israel is a chapter heading. I'd rather be part of a chapter heading than part of a footnote."

He would rather, perhaps, write the chapter. He is a talker, but he is also a doer. In 1995, he was involved in leading 1,000 settlers in the illegal expansion of Efrat.

"I was arrested for incitement and insurrection," he wrote in *The Jerusalem Post,* where he has a weekly column, "and it was only as a result of intense pressure from the U.S. that I was released after twelve difficult hours." He aligns his actions with a powerful lineage. "Our method of passive resistance and civil disobedience is in the time-honored tradition of Socrates, Thoreau, and the Rev. Martin Luther King."

One of the stated goals of the action was to demonstrate the difficulty of evacuating settlers from the West Bank and Gaza, a move considered a prerequisite for creating a contiguous Palestinian state. "If it is so problematic to remove settlers from a barren hill (it took 600 soldiers nine hours, because so many of them identify with us), how much more problematic will it be to remove settlers from their homes?" Riskin wrote.

We pull up in front of a religious college for women, where Riskin is scheduled to teach a class for overseas students. He hops out. I try to open my door, but it won't budge.

"Push harder," says David, the driver.

The US$200,000 vehicle is bombproof as well as bulletproof. "It was a gift from American supporters concerned about my safety," Riskin says. ("The Arabs don't have to live like this," David will later tell me. "They can drive wherever they want. We have to live like this.") It is only when I shove with all my strength that I manage to open the door, so heavily reinforced it makes me think of a bunker or the steel door to an isolation cell.

Rabbi Riskin sweeps into a cavernous classroom full of chattering young women. He starts talking without missing a beat. The young women turn toward him, falling silent. They are mostly American girls in their late teens, clean-scrubbed and wholesome, favouring long denim skirts, Birkenstocks with sports socks, colourful sweatshirts and hoodies. The walls of the room are lined with books, all of them religious texts. The subject of his lecture is intriguing: "The implications of the war on terror for us as Jews."

Mostly, though, the title seems a ploy to get the girls to pay attention to a lecture on Torah. Riskin talks about Noah. Why did God bring about the flood? "Because the land was filled with terror. Like now—Hamas, Arafat."

Noah took 120 years to build the Ark, he tells the class. "Unless you have Israeli *kablanim* [contractors], it shouldn't take one hundred and twenty years. But," he says, grinning and puncturing the air with his index finger, "Israeli kablanim build *very quickly in Efrat.*"

In fact, they don't. There may be an Israeli contractor somewhere in the process, but Efrat is being built by Palestinians. While walking to Riskin's office, I had asked some builders for directions. The first man didn't understand Hebrew. He called to an older man, who pointed me on my way.

"What do you think of working for a settlement?" I asked the older man.

He pushed himself back from the ledge he was leaning on. Behind his eyes, something snapped shut.

"*Caha,*" he said, which can mean both "It's like this" and "So-so."

"No problem," he added. Meaning he didn't want any, nor did he wish to make any.

"Religion is not automatically good. God is not automatically good,"

Rabbi Riskin is saying to the girls. Occasionally, he glances at his watch. "The world is now divided between those who believe in a God of compassion and justice and those who believe in Islamic fundamentalism."

He moves on to Sodom and Gomorrah, the cities of licentiousness that God pelted with fire and brimstone because there were not even ten righteous souls worth saving, despite the pleas of a soft-hearted Abraham. Yet soft-hearted as he was, "Abraham didn't make an anti-terror coalition with Sodom," explains Riskin, "because Abraham understood Sodom wasn't a freedom-loving democracy.

"From the time of Adam and Eve, the world has descended into Hamas, into terror. But one place did not forget. And that was *Eretz Israel*. Israel never forgot ethical monotheism." That's why, he continues, returning to Noah, the floods did not destroy Israel. "God guarantees victory."

He finishes with a story that, on the surface, seems completely unrelated. It is the story of a man who built a synagogue in Sydney, Australia, which Riskin was invited to dedicate. The man had had no prior interest in religion. The man's father had died in Auschwitz; it was understandably hard to believe in God. And the man had never known how or when his father had died.

One day, the man's son took a Passover trip to Phoenix—there are vacation packages for Passover in Acapulco, Passover in Hawaii, Rabbi Riskin explains—and was called to the hotel lobby for a message. It turned out the message was for an older man of the same name, and the two started talking. The older man, it emerged, had lived in the same village as the young man's grandfather. Had been sent with him to Auschwitz. Had seen the young man's grandfather die. The Jews entering Auschwitz were greeted by an orchestra, he told the young man. They were told to put their belongings onto a conveyor belt. Many had family albums, other belongings, but this young man's grandfather had only a paper bag. At first he refused to part with it.

"*Schweinhund!*" Rabbi Riskin shouts.

This is what the German guard had shouted. So the man put his paper bag on the conveyor belt. And then he picked it up again. With that, the German guard shot him in the head. The man in the hotel in Phoenix, the one who had survived, looked to see what was in the bag. "It was tefillin." The black leather boxes with straps worn by observant Jewish men in prayer.

The young man went home and told his father how and when the grandfather had died, and the father decided to build a house of prayer in his own father's memory.

And that is how Rabbi Riskin finishes his talk. He is out the door and halfway to the top of the stairs before I can catch up.

What do the girls draw from this lecture? The twin vines of politics and religion, good and evil, Hamas and the Holocaust, are intertwined in a way that is emotional rather than academic, obfuscating rather than enlightening. But they do learn one thing: "God guarantees victory." Just not for everyone.

The rabbi must be off, but he hasn't yet managed to find time for our interview. We agree to meet for dinner after his rabbinical class.

ON RABBI RISKIN'S ADVICE, I meet with Nadia Matar, a resident of Efrat and an official of the Women in Green, a settler activist group that opposes ceding any land to the Palestinians. Matar, at thirty-five, has been fondly referred to as "the settlers' Joan of Arc."

Like Shlomo Riskin, Nadia Matar is exceptionally busy. She sleeps just three hours a night. She must schedule and reschedule our meeting. Matar, who emigrated from Belgium in her late teens and married an American-born doctor, does not believe in co-existence. "I adopt the slogan of the left," she says. "Two states for two people." The Palestinian state would be in Hashemite Jordan.

Matar owns a pistol and wears a long skirt and a New York baseball cap. The host of her own settler radio show, she is accustomed to airing her views. As we speak, she barely pauses to breathe between sentences.

Each Sunday, she leads the Women in Green in protests outside the prime minister's office in Jerusalem, banging pots and shouting to disturb the weekly cabinet meeting.

"I like to say we can't give away Judea, Samaria, Gaza, Hebron and Efrat because of my earrings." She shows me the two round discs, explaining that they are coins from the Second Temple Period, after which the Jews were exiled and spread throughout the Diaspora. "If you give away Hebron, you give away your moral right to Tel Aviv, which is a conquered Arab village."

As far as I have learned, Tel Aviv was built on sand dunes, not a conquered Arab village. Matar's muddying of history sounds like a familiar attempt to extend the settler umbrella to all Israelis, thereby legitimizing the settlers' actions. To move away from circular arguments about who has the greater historical ties to ancient lands—questions as fruitless and ephemeral as who loves more, who feels more deeply—I borrow a question from David Grossman, who surveyed the terrain of the occupation, then in its twentieth year, for his prophetic book, *The Yellow Wind*. Grossman asked the settlers he visited what would be the most hateful aspect of the occupation for them if they were Palestinian.

For me, I surmise, it would be the loss of opportunity, the chance to study and find fulfilling work. For Palestinians, to dream must be painful, infused with the knowledge that their dreams will not be realized. I ask Matar, a mother of three, what she would find most difficult as a Palestinian mother.

Grossman's subjects were unanimous in their inability to formulate an answer to his question—they found it impossible to accommodate the shift in viewpoint. Matar, for the first time, pauses before speaking.

"I can't answer that question," she says. "I can't put myself in the shoes of a Palestinian mother because I see her as my enemy."

And then she says something else, something that underscores the way the conflict has devolved, for some players, into a zero-sum game. "In the law of the jungle, only the strong survive. And we will survive."

IN THE FOYER WHERE RABBI RISKIN and I are to reconnect, a security guard pounds on the Pepsi machine that has eaten his shekels while rabbinical students pace back and forth, talking into cell phones. By the end of the rabbi's class, a group has gathered to talk to him. When he manages to extricate himself we head outside, where a second car with a fresh driver is waiting. Riskin makes phone calls from the car, something to do with money. The line he wants to reach, in Florida, is busy.

We eat at an empty restaurant nearby. It is brightly lit and looks like an abandoned wedding hall, stackable auditorium chairs arranged around preset tables decorated with silk flower bouquets. The menu is typical Eastern European Jewish food with a few Israeli modifications. I order hummus and latkes; he has the gefilte fish and a main course.

Both of us feel slightly uncomfortable to find the restaurant so deserted. We run through the reasons many restaurants are lacking patrons: the dearth of tourists, fear of suicide bombings, the economy. In truth, it is hard for me not to connect each of these factors to the settlements and their central role in the ongoing conflict. "The settlements are one of the deepest injuries in the Palestinian heart," Bassem Eid, director of the Palestinian Human Rights Monitoring Group, had told me at his East Jerusalem office.

In the late 1970s, Rabbi Riskin says, outlining the journey that has brought him to Efrat, he was visiting Israel when a man named Moshe Moskovitz took him to the top of a hill overlooking Jerusalem. "He had a dream to build a town," says Riskin. "He quoted Dizengoff, the first mayor of Tel Aviv. Someone asked Dizengoff, 'How do you become the mayor of a city?' He said, 'You build a city.' "

So a dream was born. Moskovitz would become the mayor of this new city, and Riskin its chief rabbi.

Riskin, then in his thirties, founded an organization called "The Beginning of Redemption." The name underscores the end goal of religious settlers: to prepare the way for the Messiah by placing Greater Israel—all of traditional Palestine, including the territories—in Jewish hands. The ground-breaking ceremony took place in 1981 with Ariel Sharon in attendance. In 1983, Riskin, his wife, their four children and 190 families involved with The Beginning of Redemption immigrated to Israel and moved to Efrat.

But why the territories? Why not Jerusalem?

"We have one homeland. This is our homeland. Jews have lived here in an unbroken chain for 4,000 years."

So have Arabs, I remind him.

"Look," he says, "we have good relations with the Arabs. You are usually safer by having good relations, because they have something to lose." The settlers don't want to take anyone's land, he says. They want to share it.

My hummus arrives. I offer to share it and he takes a small sampling but says he is watching his weight.

Riskin was originally in favour of negotiations and a sovereign Palestinian state. In the years after Oslo he began to sour. "We were giving up land and we were arming the Palestinians. And there were terrorist attacks. It moved me to the right. And I saw what Arafat was doing to my Arab friends. We used to have basketball games every week. He stopped it. We were sending Arab women for early childhood education classes. He stopped it. But the worst came a year ago. And now this war of ours is not about Judea and Samaria, it's about the right of Jews to have any state at all. For me, this is as white and black a struggle as you can get."

In a speech Rabbi Riskin delivered at Cornell University in 2001, sponsored by the Center for Jewish Living, he expressed the same senti-ment in different words. "Occupation is wrong," he was quoted as say-ing in the *Cornell Daily Sun*. "But we face a choice between being the occupier or the 'occupyee'—and I would choose being the occupier."

About the situation for Palestinians living under occupation, he tells me, "I have very little sympathy. I buried three Efratis this year. I buried a little boy whose face couldn't be identified; they had to identify him by his teeth. I have no sympathy. They want to throw us into the sea! The Palestinian Authority are evil, ruthless terrorists that have to be destroyed. Look at the poor people bombed in Dresden. What a tragedy! Not a tragedy at all. The Nazis wanted to destroy *me.*"

Is he aware of the conditions under which Palestinians are living?

"But it's *got to be.* It's *got to be.*" He cites this week's drive-by shooting in the West Bank in which four Israeli women were killed by Palestinian gunmen. I mention a drive-by shooting the previous week in which six Palestinians were injured by a group of unidentified Jewish settlers. Israeli security forces believe this same squad may be responsible for five or six other such incidents and a dozen Palestinian deaths.

"These were fringe elements who did what was condemned by all," Riskin insists, echoing the official Palestinian response to their own militants. He wants to see Arafat pushed "to the brink," even if that means a more radical leadership, such as the militant Islamic group Hamas, takes his place. For him, groups such as Hamas and the Palestinian Authority are one and the same. Still, he says, he believes in a Palestinian state.

Are the settlements complicating matters if negotiations must eventually set borders? I ask.

"Why borders? I think the area can be shared very fairly. It should be a co-operation. Like the European Union."

The EU members have defined borders, I point out.

"Look, the first law in dealing with terrorists is you can't give them a prize for terrorism."

I make the suggestion that without Jewish terrorist groups like Lehi (the Stern Gang) or Etzel (Irgun), Israel might never have driven out the British and created an independent state.

"We never targeted civilians," he replies without pausing. And the civilians killed in Bethlehem last week—at least eleven, according to the Israeli human rights group B'Tselem—in the army incursion that followed the assassination of Israel's tourism minister? "That's their fault."

I am at a loss for words. All of my remaining questions dissipate like smoke. Riskin is a swift, smooth talker, and I can almost believe that *he* believes the settlements are good for his Arab neighbours, that he wants to share, that he wishes for peace. His, it would seem, is a benevolent form of colonialism. But his words and his actions move in opposite directions. And he, too, has become bulletproof: nothing penetrates.

David Grossman, in the course of writing his book, visited well-spoken, moderate settlers like Riskin, whom Grossman says are put on display, and the unrestrained, like those who supported the Jewish underground, which in the 1980s planted bombs in the cars of several Arab mayors, blowing off the foot of one, the legs of another. The militant group went on to plant bombs on Arab busses, shoot up an Islamic university, and make a break-in attempt armed with dynamite at the Jerusalem mosque known as the Dome of the Rock, the Muslim holy site that stands where the Jewish Temple once stood. Most had their sentences commuted due to vast outpourings of support, demonstrations and petitions. Even today they are viewed as heroes by some right-wing Israelis, much as the *shahids* (martyrs) are venerated in Palestinian society for suicide bombings.

At one time, Grossman writes, messianic definitions of a Greater Israel seemed "daydreams disconnected from reality." No more. The dreamers and their supporters must be given serious attention, he argues. "They, after all, see the Bible as an operational order. An operation that, even if its time is yet to come, will come and, if it does not come soon enough, will need to be brought." For Riskin, the settlements may be the "beginning of redemption"—but I find myself wondering where it will end.

Outside the empty restaurant, Rabbi Riskin's vehicles have changed again. David is back, waiting in the suv to drive Riskin to his next class. While David drives, Riskin counsels a woman by cell phone.

"Susan, Susan, Susan," he says. "Ninety per cent of the second marriages I deal with have prenuptial agreements. You can marry him or not marry him. Listen, you can even renegotiate the prenuptial. But you can't lock a man out of his own home."

He leaves, and David drives me to the Jerusalem bus station. All at once it becomes clear that David has taken a shine to me. He reaches back over the front seat and grasps my hand in his enormous paw. He kisses it, grazing it with his bristling black beard.

I tell him no and pull away. We are flying through the Jerusalem night and I am in the back seat, sitting as far from him as I can. He lifts his eyes from the road, reaches out again and grabs my face roughly, trying to pull me toward him. There is no attempt at subtlety or seduction. I resist, feeling alarmed but not yet frightened. He turns onto a deserted road that I do not recognize, and for an instant I believe this will turn out very badly, but then we are on the main road again, surrounded by traffic. At the bus station, I wrestle away from his determined embrace and shove open the reinforced door. It is only on the bus to Tel Aviv, surrounded by sleepy soldiers, that my heart stops pounding.

For all the nice talk of sharing, of "Arab friends," of basketball games and the education of the native population, it seems many settlers have come to believe they are within their rights to reach out and take whatever they want. This sense of entitlement cannot help but infect other aspects of their lives. The boundary between fantasy—dreams, wishes, visions—and reality has been transgressed. Some notion of restraint or the sanctity of what belongs to the other has been lost in the process.

I recall Rabbi Riskin's remark on the phone, and it occurs to me that you *can* lock a man out of his own home. You can force a man from his land; you can demolish the house he lives in. It is happening, in part, because of men like Riskin, who believe that they hold a divinely procured land title. That victory is theirs, guaranteed.

CHAPTER 8

Postcards from Ramallah

The Muslim Quarter after Ramadan prayers, Jerusalem

THE FARTHER WE go into Jerusalem's Muslim Quarter, the more relentlessly crowded it becomes. Candace spots openings in the sea of people and jets her small-hipped frame through them. She has started working for the United Nations Development Programme in East Jerusalem. Today is her day off, and we have planned to visit the West Bank city of Ramallah.

We find a shared taxi at Damascus Gate to take us the fifteen-minute journey to Kalandia, the checkpoint between Jerusalem and Ramallah. Parked vehicles line the road as we near the checkpoint; some are luxury cars, Mercedes and the like, whose owners walk across rather than

wait out the excruciating lineups. Other cars and delivery trucks sim-
mer in the sun for hours as they wait to be searched by armed soldiers.
The taxi driver weaves through traffic and takes us as close as he can,
then everyone disembarks and walks across to find another taxi on the
other side.

There is the sound of horns and engines, the smell of exhaust fumes,
dust, heat, impatience. Everything, everyone, looks faded. Cement
blocks have been set up to prevent vehicles from breaking rank and
ploughing down soldiers. Some enterprising types have struck up busi-
nesses, selling ice cream or snacks car to car.

On the taxi ride to Ramallah, we drive past several armed Palestinian
guards. "Do you know how to tell a Kalashnikov from an m-16?" asks
Candace.

She enlightens me, pointing out the Kalashnikov's distinctive curved
magazine.

A young man in a cherry-red convertible speeds past us on the
shoulder of the road and burns around a corner. Before the Israeli occupation, when Jordan controlled the West Bank, Ramallah was a popular
vacation spot for wealthy Jordanians who wanted a break from the heat
of Amman. Now, Ramallah is part of Area A, run by the Palestinian
Authority. "There's still a lot of money in this town," Candace says.

The taxi lets us off in Ramallah's Manara Square in the centre of
town. A huge Coca-Cola billboard looms overhead, almost comforting
in its familiarity. Plastered on a building below it is an equally large
poster of a young, gentle-faced man. But he is not as gentle as he looks.
In many places, on walls and pasted over billboards, are smaller posters
of other young men, "martyrs," some of them suicide bombers.

Arabic newspapers are stacked at the kiosks. They feature front-page
pictures of George W. Bush and Colin Powell, both looking caught in
the headlights. The photographs of Arafat show him smiling, embrac-
ing a visiting dignitary. A British cartographer I met at the hospice told
me she thinks Arabic and Hebrew newspapers mirror one another: the

Arabic papers say the Jews want Arabs deported; the Hebrew papers say the Arabs want to drive Jews into the sea.

I stop on the sidewalk to photograph a man making flat bread on a convex grill. His friend interrupts. "No picture." He wags a finger.

"Why not?" I say.

"No picture," he says sternly.

I explain that I'm a tourist. Why no picture?

"Intifada," he says.

I suspect he is worried I am taking photographs for military purposes, perhaps to show to the Shin Bet, Israel's secret service, so they can find some way to turn his friend into a collaborator. Everyone here is a little paranoid. I take pains to avoid an accidental slippage into Hebrew, a "*slichah*"—"excuse me"—on the bustling streets.

Candace and I walk past the police station where two Israeli soldiers were torn to pieces last year by an angry mob. Most of the station has been bombed to hell, but on the outer wall, in red spray paint, someone has written, "A settler a day keeps the doctor away." Inside the compound is the husk of a car.

We wander down another, more tranquil street, past a beautiful stone house with turquoise shutters.

"Yasser Arafat's mother-in-law lives in Ramallah," offers Candace. "I've heard she has a BMW parked outside her house."

Money that goes to the Palestinian Authority is known to filter down to friends and family. Corruption is a common, well-founded complaint. We look at the house, wondering if this could be the one belonging to Arafat's mother-in-law. No BMW, however.

Farther down the same street we arrive at Birzeit University's Democracy and Workers' Rights Center. We walk inside and introduce ourselves to a man with a small moustache. I ask if we can talk to someone. He disappears for a moment, leaving us to look through a shelf full of Arabic publications and postcards of homes demolished by the Israel Defense Forces (IDF). The most recent packet of postcards is called

"Evidence." These are photographs of Palestinians boys, most in their early teens, who have been shot in the chest or between the eyes. Not the kind of postcards you'd send home.

The man emerges from the inner offices and invites us to follow him. We are introduced to Carine Metz, the centre's Legal Advisor on Economic, Social and Cultural Rights, and Wajih Al-Ayassa, Director of Education and Training. The four of us sit in their unadorned office as Metz and Al-Ayassa tell us that the median income in Gaza and the West Bank has plunged by half in the past year. "The closures have a double effect," says Metz, a bright-eyed young woman, referring to the practice of sealing off Palestinian villages with checkpoints and roadblocks. "They forbid Palestinian workers to go to Israel to work and at the same time forbid Palestinians to import raw materials."

But that's only part of the frustration. Al-Ayassa, who lives in Bethlehem, says it takes him up to three hours to get to work in Ramallah. Sometimes, he doesn't arrive at all. The round-trip taxi fare (few Palestinians bother driving cars any more because so many roads are restricted or blocked) is 34 shekels. Workers earning 1,000 shekels a month who must spend 600 of that on taxis find it hard to rationalize holding on to their jobs.

Even with the many problems, Metz and Al-Ayassa think life under the Palestinian Authority has been an improvement over life under direct occupation. "You can work on your infrastructure," says Al-Ayassa. "You can work on changing your laws."

Al-Ayassa pours strong coffee from his thermos into tiny plastic cups. As he becomes more comfortable, his English grows fluent. He gives us an overview of the legal system in the occupied territories. The West Bank is governed by British Mandate law, Jordanian law carried over from before 1967 and Israeli military law. Gaza is governed by British Mandate law, Egyptian law from before 1967 and Israeli military law. Both territories also come under laws carried over from the time of Ottoman rule, which ended in 1917. Because Israeli military law is only applied "when it's in Israeli interests, like the use of water and who can drill wells," Al-Ayassa says, "we've become alienated. We don't trust the law."

"Israeli occupation orders are imposed on us," adds Metz. "This has created a climate that is a kind of lawlessness. People in the West think that Israel is a democracy. It is far more complex than that.

"Palestinians are waiting for the fruits of the peace process. After 1996, they became tired. They didn't see an end to the settlements; they saw more settlements. Even workers with permits didn't see their situation improve. Now, we hear about pregnant women giving birth at checkpoints. The soldiers don't allow them to cross to get to the hospital. The more people suffer, the more they become desperate. If there is no justice, you do justice yourself. When you have a proper justice system, you don't have to do it yourself. But the IDF is not accepting complaints from Palestinians."

Lately, it has become prohibitively expensive to live in the centre of Ramallah, Metz says, where it is safest. There is a better chance of finding housing in areas where the shelling is heaviest. Metz has learned to sleep through the shooting, but she avoids windows. One night she slept in her staircase. "One bullet is enough," she says, noting that a local man was killed in his home while watching the events of September 11 with his family on their television.

Al-Ayassa talks about the number of deaths during the current intifada. The Palestinian death toll outnumbers that of Israelis by three or four times. "We have problems with the Western media because they think that after Oslo we have peace and a state. They don't understand that we don't have the authority to control our own lives. If an Israeli settler goes to live in the occupied territories, people have a right to defend themselves. This is occupied territory, and the settlements are illegal."

Much of the centre's work involves defending workers' rights. Now, with the supply of Palestinian workers far exceeding demand, salaries are being driven down. Unemployment in the occupied territories is around 50 per cent. Already, in some towns, it is as high as 90. "Unemployment increases extremism," says Al-Ayassa.

Creating adequate labour laws is difficult, not least because Palestinian leaders do not consider more stringent standards to be in their economic interest. Even the United Nations has tried to take advantage of the labour climate. According to the centre's annual report, 700 employees and contract workers at the United Nations Relief and Works Agency (UNRWA) received notice in the year 2000 that new contracts were to offer wages 30 to 35 per cent below existing ones. Anyone refusing to sign the new contracts would be dismissed. With lost benefits factored in, the potential decline in wages was calculated by the centre to be 55 per cent. Actions by the centre's legal unit, who advised workers not to sign the new agreement, succeeded in freezing the previous contracts.

I mention the influx of foreign workers I've noticed around the country: the Filipino maids, Thai builders, Romanian workers crowding into Christian shrines on their days off. Metz says these people are brought in to do the work Palestinians used to do. "They can be sent back after two or three years. They don't have the same history. So they are easier to control."

Metz and Al-Ayassa say there is almost nothing in the way of a self-sufficient economy within Palestinian society. Palestinians have long depended on Israel for work and trade. Now, most work permits for Palestinians have been cut off. Those who still have them consider them "like gold," Metz tells us.

On the way back through town, Candace and I pass the local movie theatre, where *Gladiator* and a forgettable Antonio Banderas vehicle are playing. Above the movie ads are posters of Yasser Arafat, plastered one beside the other. We have trouble finding a taxi going in the right direction, so we ask a policeman. He flags one down in the middle of Manara Square, blocking traffic. While Candace gets in, I run to photograph a wall mural, a red bird bearing what I now recognize as a Kalashnikov.

At the Kalandia checkpoint, we step out of the taxi and walk past two Israeli soldiers. They are so happy to see two blonde women that they ignore the cars trying to get through and come over to talk to us. Their commander is enraged. He shouts at them from a distance, but these particular soldiers are winding up their service in a few weeks, they tell us. They ignore him.

The soldiers seem bored with their work, but resigned. "There's not much action now," shrugs Itai. He urges me to travel to Eilat, Israel's party town of surf and sun, rather than wasting my time in a dust pit like Kalandia. "You shouldn't be here," he says. "It's not safe. But it's nice for us. It improves the scenery."

It wouldn't take much to do that. The checkpoint is a wasteland of rubble and garbage, diesel fumes, gridlock, despair. Candace and I leave them to their work and find a taxi to drive us to Jerusalem. A small car parked near the checkpoint has a sign in the back that reads, in English: "Thank You for Being Safety." I ponder its message all the way to Damascus Gate.

CHAPTER 9

The Sound of Music

The Western Wall and Dome of the Rock, Jerusalem

THE COMMONWEALTH seals on the passports Candace and I hold ease our passage through the Israeli checkpoint between Jerusalem and the West Bank town of Bethlehem. We have arranged to meet Candace's friend Roma, a university student majoring in business administration.

With her glossy hair and enormous dark eyes, twenty-one-year-old Roma is possibly the most beautiful girl in Bethlehem, if not the entire West Bank. A Palestinian Christian who, like everyone in her family, is fluent in five languages (Arabic, Greek, Hebrew, French and English), Roma has been offered a scholarship to study in Italy. She speaks of trying to transfer it to her younger brother, Elias, who wants to be a fashion designer when he graduates from high school.

Candace and I are sitting around the table with Roma and her family, eating a lunch of lamb and rice, when a volley of gunfire erupts outside their home. Everyone is on instant alert. This is why the family abandoned their house for a week and went to live with relatives—they have only just moved back. Elias runs outside to make sure all the neighbour children are accounted for. I run to the balcony in a foolish attempt to see where the shooting is taking place.

Seven-year-old Lydia, the youngest sister, buries her face in the living room sofa, in tears. She is crying because she misses her friend Johnny, her parents tell me. Johnny is the seventeen-year-old altar boy shot not long ago outside the nearby Church of the Nativity. Now whenever Lydia hears gunfire, she thinks of Johnny, and cries.

Roma's mother turns up the stereo. She is animated, pretty like her daughters. She consoles Lydia, tries to distract her by convincing her to dance. "This is our life," says their father, a dentist. "This is how we live." "This is our *Sound of Music*," says a visiting aunt, as the shooting continues outside.

We return to the table. More food all around, oranges and chocolate. Eat, eat, the family urges, eat. Eating is a way to drown the anger, they say. More wine. They break out a bottle of Cypriot brandy; even the children get a shot in their Turkish coffee. The demitasse cups are decorated with funny faces. "So you never have to drink alone," jokes the uncle, a distinguished-looking man in a neat grey suit. Lydia, up from the sofa now, is laughing.

Roma's uncle lives near Jerusalem. To get permission to travel for this one-day family visit, held to commemorate the anniversary of an elderly relative's death, he and his wife lied to Israeli authorities, showing papers for a family house in Bethlehem and saying it was their own. The uncle was born in Ramle, a town between Jerusalem and Tel Aviv, where his father owned olive groves and olive presses. One day in 1948, his father disappeared. For nine months, no one in the family knew the father had been taken prisoner by the Israeli armed forces for use in a prisoner exchange—a hundred Arabs for every Jew. When Israel's Prime Minister David Ben-Gurion ordered the expulsion of 50,000 Arab residents of Ramle and Lod (an event written about by Yitzhak Rabin), the uncle's mother obeyed the soldiers' orders, locked the doors to their house, left everything behind and walked with her son to Ramallah.

Roma's father, the uncle's brother-in-law, is no longer allowed to visit Jerusalem. He is quiet and observant, but his voice rises as he speaks of the travel restrictions. "Jerusalem is six kilometres from here. I can't go there. I can't pass the checkpoint without permission. It's been five years!" In Arabic, he adds, "We will all go to jail if they hear us talking."

The children listen for the gunfire to stop. The moment they are certain it is over, they will race outside to collect the bullet casings. They are like kids everywhere with their collecting crazes. They fill large plastic bottles with the spent bullets; one of the cousins has already shown me his, hoisting it onto his shoulder. It is hard to carry, like a bottle full of coins.

"Of course it is temporary," says the uncle, in response to something I ask. "The question is, how long will it last? Fifty years in the life of a country is nothing. But even a month for a human being is long."

A chubby neighbour boy of about twelve bursts into the house. The coast is clear, he informs the other children. The boy wears a talisman around his neck—a bullet the length of my hand, the kind the children call a "500." He also wears around his neck, in a plastic frame, a photograph of Atef Abayat, until recently the leading local fighter. Abayat cuts a handsome figure, as soldiers will. He was assassinated not long ago, along with two companions, in a car bombing orchestrated by Israel.

At Bethlehem University, Roma tells me, students tattoo Abayat's image on their arms. "They loved him because he was so nice," she says. I write down his name in my green notebook, and the family worries aloud that I will be arrested for doing so. I have a press card, I tell them, knowing they are the ones who should worry, wondering if I should blacken out their names in my notes.

Roma's mother pulls out an envelope containing Lydia's schoolwork. The teacher has asked the children to draw whatever they want, and Lydia has drawn a sketch of men beating other men with clubs, a child throwing a rock at a tank, a police cruiser and an F-16 fighter bomber marked with a Star of David. I write down what I see in this single picture. Lydia, who is beside me on a chair, leans her face to my ear. "Are you writing about Atef Abayat?" she whispers.

The other children rush in, breathless, bearing their souvenir bullets. The uncle's oldest son, not yet a teen, shows off today's trophy: a 500. "Can we come next weekend to collect more?" the boy implores.

"We have our next weekend planned," sighs the uncle, an indulgent parent. He knows they won't be able to return to Bethlehem next weekend, or for a long time after that. His younger daughter, a pale redhead, shows him her bullets, too. One has a silver centre, one a bronze. To me he says, "You ask 99 per cent of people what they wish, they will say good times for the next generation."

I sit next to Roma, whose presence fills the room. She likes to dance, to laugh, to eat chocolate. She eats eight Snickers bars a day, she confesses, starting when she wakes up at 3:00 a.m. to study and then one for each university lecture, but she somehow manages to stay slim. The doctor told her she is nervous, that's why she burns it off—"Thanks to God," she says, laughing—but he has advised her to cut back.

Some of Roma's fellow students come to Bethlehem from Jerusalem or Ramallah. They lie to the soldiers and say they are going to work; otherwise, they may be forbidden to pass. Students, who played a central role in the first intifada, are viewed with suspicion by the army. Many leave home at 6:00 a.m. for 8:00 a.m lectures, but due to roadblocks and checkpoints they sometimes don't arrive till 10:30. "They are tired, hungry, they have been walking through the mud," Roma says. "They don't have a mind for studies. They must sit and eat something, have a coffee.

They leave to go home at five o'clock and arrive at eight or nine. There is no time to study. They wonder why they even bothered."

She tells me that Bethlehem University considered cancelling the fall semester due to all the teaching time the closures had cost. But the students pleaded with administrators to extend the semester for as long as it took them to finish.

This past summer Roma went to a party, her first in a year and a half. "I used to go to four parties a week, wear four different dresses, four different hairstyles," she says, laughing. Now, except to attend classes, she never goes out. She prefers to stay inside, close to her family, and her family prefers that too. Everyone is home by five. "No place is safe," says Roma. "You become addicted to staying in."

Later, Elias shows me the party dresses he has made for Roma—emerald greens, sapphire blues, low-cut, sexy. He laments that the local Muslim girls wear only shapeless robes. Then it's time to turn on the family's favourite soap, *The Bold and the Beautiful.* Any excuse to escape the reality outside their door.

The phone rings, and Elias gets up to answer. A neighbour is calling to say that a thirteen-year-old boy from Bethlehem has just been killed by the gunfire. *The Bold and the Beautiful* is temporarily adjourned. The news comes on, pictures of a young boy in a hospital bed, tubes emerging from his body, but in any case too late. The Israeli media will allege that he had been throwing rocks.

Elias sits near me, perched on the edge of the sofa. On the walls around us are pictures of the Last Supper, the Virgin Mary. Elias starts to talk, and the words pour out. He knows he needs to leave here, knows there is no future for him in Bethlehem. "What does Palestine need with a fashion designer?" says his uncle solemnly, and Elias nods, agreeing. Elias doesn't like school, doesn't like his studies, doesn't care about any of it. "I talk too much," he says suddenly, as his words tumble over one another. "But I need to talk to someone. Roma is always studying, my mother is running around, my father is working—well, trying to work—

and I am in my room. Sometimes I talk to myself. Sometimes I cry. I can't even go out and buy an ice cream because of this whole situation."

He goes to the room he still shares with Roma and comes back with a beautiful embroidery, suitable for a bookmark or a small wall hanging. "My sister taught me how," he says. "You have it. It's for you."

I hold the delicate swath of fabric in my hand. Study the scarlet flowers against the black background.

It will be dark soon. Someone arranges for a taxi. The driver's small son sits on the armrest in the front seat next to his father, who drives Candace and me to the checkpoint. We walk through and, finding no taxis on the other side, stand by the roadside to hitch a ride the rest of the way.

Two Palestinian Christian businessmen in a Mercedes stop to pick us up. The driver shows us the pass from a South American embassy that allows him to navigate the checkpoints. The man in the passenger seat runs a souvenir shop in Bethlehem. Business is predictably terrible. He worked for peace in the late 1980s, he tells us, but "the Palestinians made many mistakes," such as resorting to violence to further their cause. It played poorly in the Western media. Now, he has no hope for peace. No hope but one: "The Lord will come back soon, and He will reign."

As dusk falls over Jerusalem, a Jewish girl in modest religious attire crosses the street in front of the Mercedes. The light changes and the traffic moves, slowly, erratically, bearing us along.

Land of the Sad Oranges

Schoolgirls, Gaza City

*T*HE BUS FROM THE Israeli town of Ashkelon is packed with young soldiers, male and female, likely headed to the same place I am. I get off at the stop nearest to Erez crossing, the border between Israel and the Gaza Strip. A grizzled Israeli in a jean jacket, with a snowy beard, disembarks at the same stop, accompanied by a teenaged boy.

I ask the man if he knows how to get to Gaza. In Israel, "go to Gaza" (*lech le'Aza*) is another way of saying "go to hell"(*lech le'azazel*), and I can tell from his stricken expression that I may as well have named that as my destination.

"It's okay," I say. "It's quiet."

"The graveyards are full of people who said that," he replies.

We wait at a hitchhiking post. It is noon under a warm November sun. There are no other busses passing this way, and I have no idea how much farther it is to Erez or if I will make it today. A few cars drive past, followed by extended periods of silence and empty road. A soldier joins us, lights a cigarette, goes and stands a distance away.

The landscape is dry desert. It feels like the last exit to nowhere. I pass the time by trying to gauge how big a mistake I have made in coming here. What impressions I have of the Gaza Strip have come largely via the TV screen. The disturbing scene of young Mohammad al-Durrah dying in his father's arms last year is one of the few images that I, and much of the world, carry of the place.

"You have been to Scarborough?" asks the man with the white beard, who has gathered that I am Canadian.

"No."

"Tst-tst-tst." He clucks his tongue. "You have been to Alaska?"

"No."

"Tst-tst-tst. You have been to the Yukon?"

No, near to it, but not exactly.

"Tst-tst-tst," he says, shaking his head. It seems I am failing all his tests of civilized society. Plus, I am going to Gaza. There is little hope for me now.

A car approaches and pulls over. I pile in after the man and the teenaged boy. The driver lets me off a few minutes down the road at a sign pointing to Erez. The last thing I hear before slamming the door is the older man shouting to me, "Give me your parents' number so I can inform them when you don't come back."

Hauling my daypack onto my shoulder, I follow the arrow on the sign that reads " 'Safe Passage' to Gaza." The quotation marks around "Safe Passage" make it sound tongue-in-cheek. The road, two lanes in each direction, is deserted. The wind whistles past my ears as I contemplate how long it would take for someone to find me if I was shot here. An hour? A day?

In another five minutes I round a corner and come upon an enormous border crossing, eerie in its vast emptiness. To one side are the narrow passageways where Palestinians line up to cross into Israel and ride the bus to their low-wage jobs, trimming hedges or painting houses or washing dishes in tourist hotels. Between 1970 and 1987, the number of Gazans earning money inside Israel rose from 10 per cent to at least 60 per cent of the work force. The money bought refrigerators and television sets, but created no independent economic infrastructure. After Gaza was hermetically fenced in 1991, the closures began, meaning that only the rare Gazan holding a coveted work permit may come or go. A quarter of a million foreign workers have since entered Israel to replace Palestinian labour. In 2002, the Israeli army will spend a quarter of a billion shekels (US$100 million) on Gaza's fences and military outposts.

I spot the customs office and enter. The building is clean and modern. I ask the soldier checking my passport if things are quiet.

"Yes, thank God," he says.

Two burly Danes having their passports examined are the only other non-employees in the office. Hoping they will care to split a taxi, I ask if they are heading to Gaza City, but they are travelling in the opposite direction. "To Ben-Gurion Airport," one says.

Guest pass in hand, I hike the quarter-kilometre to the Palestinian side, past the cement barriers and the trio of Israeli soldiers holed up inside the final checkpoint, feasting on sandwiches. The Palestinian checkpoint is a shack where three guards sit under a picture of Arafat and a poster of a small boy preparing to hurl a stone at an Israeli tank. The soldiers are smoking cigarettes and talking to an older, white-haired man, who is neatly dressed in civilian clothes. The man speaks English, and I ask him how much I should pay for a taxi to Gaza City.

"Well, you should barter," he says. "But keep in mind that the economy here is, if you'll excuse me, fucked up."

We talk for a few moments and I ask him who he is.

"The most famous photojournalist in the world," he says.

He is meeting a team from France 2 Television. If there is room in the car, I am welcome to a ride. Palestinian taxi drivers are hovering outside expectantly. One of the soldiers goes out to yell at them.

Minutes later, I am barrelling through the streets of Gaza with three journalists and a trunk full of camera equipment. The crew is already late for an interview, their cameraman having been held up at the Kalandia checkpoint outside Jerusalem. We weave between donkey carts and Mercedes, people and animals. Smoke billows from a shawarma shop. Bananas hang in enormous rippling clusters from market stalls. Water sellers drive torturously slowly, blasting electronic jingles on loudspeakers. Tel Aviv, itself a frenetic place, seems staid and lifeless by comparison.

The world's most famous photojournalist, whose name is Talal Abu Rahma, is telling Charles Enderlin, bureau chief for France 2, that the Palestinian police were shooting at Islamic Jihad members who had congregated in Gaza to protest the arrest of a member.

"Why were they shooting?" asks Charles.

"I guess they lost their dignity," says Talal.

"They had dignity to lose?"

Half an hour later we are hauling camera equipment into the new headquarters of Mohammad Dahlan, one of the leaders from the first intifada, which originated in Gaza. Dahlan is now Gaza's head of security. His 4x4 sits forlornly in the heavily guarded compound, shot full of bullet holes from a recent Israeli assassination attempt. Two holes are lodged neatly in the head rest of the passenger seat. Somehow, Dahlan survived unscathed.

Inside the main building, beefy bodyguards in boxy suits wear wires and saunter around checking our bags. All cell phones must be left outside Dahlan's office, since booby-trapped cell phones have been used in assassination attempts. From the four of us, the guards collect six.

"She works with Talal," Charles Enderlin says to Dahlan, explaining my presence.

A tall man in a pale green suit, Dahlan looks like a Latin soap opera star. "You have bad luck," he tells me, flashing a row of white teeth from behind an imposing desk. "First, because you work with Talal. Second, because you work in Gaza."

His office is furnished with overstuffed chairs, thick glass ashtrays and overwrought gold-toned tissue boxes. A TV set is tuned to the Arabic news network, Al Jazeera, which is documenting the latest fashion trend on the streets of Tokyo: the checkered black-and-white kaffiyeh worn by Yasser Arafat in the photo over Dahlan's desk. Dahlan, considered a possible successor to Arafat, has just tendered his resignation to the Palestinian Authority, but Arafat will not accept it. Dahlan is tired of arresting militants to prevent them from attacking Israel while Israel attacks him and his men. He doesn't want to put people in jail if Israel is going to bomb the jails again.

The crew is interviewing him for a documentary about the shattered peace process. Before filming, they turn the office lights down and shine a lamp in his face. "Ah," jokes Dahlan, "this is the Israeli tradition."

When the interview is over, Talal drives Enderlin and the cameraman back to Erez, where they will catch a ride to Jerusalem. I have decided to stay a few more days, but their work is done and they want to leave before the evening round of shooting starts near the border crossing. All three have been shot at one time or another, whether by rubber-coated bullets or the real thing. The cameraman, a wiry, highstrung, chain-smoking Palestinian from Jerusalem, spent two months in hospital after taking a bullet through the back. He says he is more frightened these days than he used to be.

It is already dark, so Talal lowers the windows in the car and turns on the interior lights. As we approach Erez, he switches off the headlights—"So they can see our faces."

I DECIDE TO STAY AT the Beach Hotel in Gaza City, a favourite of visiting journalists. In the lobby of the hotel, where I and a French news crew from TV 5 are the only guests, there hangs an embroidered map of the Gaza Strip inscribed, "To those who were martyred for the land of the sad oranges . . . And to those who have not been martyred yet."

Gaza was once famous for its citrus exports. These days little gets in or out except journalists. News is the main export from this sorry tract of land, measuring just forty-five kilometres by eight—and the suffering of its 1.2 million Palestinian inhabitants, two-thirds of them refugees, its main story line.

In 1948, Gaza swelled with some 200,000 refugees fleeing the war in Palestine, effectively tripling the population. In the 1967 Six-Day War, Israel wrested control of Gaza from Egypt, and soon after began constructing settlements. Today 7,000 Jewish settlers live in eighteen settlements Israel has established. Between the settlements and the army bases set up to protect them, Israel has total control of 42 per cent of Gaza's coastline, at least 20 per cent of the land, and most of the arable soil.

In *The Gaza Strip: The Political Economy of De-Development,* Harvard research associate Sara Roy asserts that Gaza has been deliberately "de-developed" by Israel through a variety of measures "including land expropriation and the expulsion of the indigenous population." She documents how attempts at economic independence and industrialization have been stymied, with international aid restricted to the provision of social services. In the eyes of Israel, an independent Palestinian economy would lead inexorably to the establishment of an independent Palestinian state.

As it stands, the population density in the Palestinian areas of Gaza is more than 3,300 inhabitants per square kilometre, among the highest in the world. Half of the population is under fifteen. Half the population lives on less than US$2 a day. Unemployment hovers at 50 per cent, far higher in some of the refugee camps. Militant Islam, like misery, is stronger in Gaza than anywhere else in the occupied territories.

"The strength of Islamism," writes Sara Roy, herself Jewish and the daughter of Holocaust survivors, "is rooted in the territory's extreme poverty, isolation, and traditional social structures, and its growth has been nourished by a profound sense of popular despair over the steady disintegration of daily life and the consistent failure of the nationalist movement to achieve any political resolution to the Palestinian-Israeli conflict and to end the occupation."

The Gaza Strip, notes Roy, has been called "the forgotten man of the Middle East," "the stepchild of the West Bank," "the black hole of the Arab world" and "Israel's collective punishment." These days Palestinians have a new name for the fenced enclosure: "the big jail." The joke goes that during the talks leading up to the Oslo Accords, the Israelis offered Gaza to the Palestinians and the Palestinians replied, "And what will you give us in return?"

ON THE SEASHORE NOT FAR from the Beach Hotel is an abandoned carnival. The Ferris wheel has rusted in the salty air. The Tilt-A-Whirl hasn't tilted or whirled in years. It is eerie to look at, the festival lights still hanging haphazardly, the entryway decorated with flaking murals showing scenes of newlyweds, excited kids, people having fun. To think that one day the carnival was running, entertaining people, and the next day all that stopped. What happened that last day? Who was the last person to glimpse the view from atop the Ferris wheel? I look over my shoulder as a donkey clomps past pulling a cart along the road behind me, the driver lifting his hand to wave.

Beyond the carnival is the Mediterranean, glistening, magnificent. Along the beach, shirtless boys balance on skiffs or stand on the shore scooping shellfish into buckets and pouring them into carts pulled by donkeys. On the side of the road, a young boy sits under a cigarette billboard selling freshly caught fish, holding up the day's catch in his hands. In the distance, Israeli ships keep silent watch.

It is a quiet news week, so Talal has offered to show me around. We meet at his Gaza City office and take his car, which has the added security of a sign for France 2 prominently displayed on the dashboard. With Mohammad Fouad, an Egyptian singer who is starting to grow on me, in the cassette player, we drive toward the Jewish settlement block of Gush Katif, passing through the Israeli-controlled junction of Abu Holi. All around the junction, the land is scarred and barren, the fields and trees torn up. Tank tracks mark the ground; the road is lined by cement barriers.

Talal tells me his family lived in Gaza prior to the refugees. Fourteen years ago, he was approached by Bob Simon, the American correspondent, on the street in Gaza. Talal was educated at a Baptist college in the United States and speaks fluent English, so Simon persuaded him to act as a fixer, arranging interviews and translating. Soon, other media outlets began calling. Today Talal works as a correspondent for France 2 and CNN.

We wait at a stoplight in front of a guard tower while settlers cross on an Israeli-only bypass road. A car from Reuters idles behind us. The soldier operating the stoplight looks out from the tower.

"Sometimes we sit here for two minutes, sometimes two hours," says Talal, watching the stoplight. Sometimes the junction, the only route to southern Gaza and the refugee camp at Khan Younis, is closed altogether.

Talal has turned off the music and lowered the windows. He is listening intently. Finally the light turns green and he noses the car ahead, but the soldier who has changed the light shouts, "Stop!" in Hebrew through the loudspeaker. Talal hits the brake. Seconds later, a white armoured settler vehicle barrels across our path.

"Go!" the soldier shouts. We go.

Had Talal not learned a rudimentary Hebrew from long-past business dealings in Tel Aviv, had he not lowered the windows, listened and understood, the consequences are easy to envision. "See, he made a mistake," says Talal. "And the story would be that he told us to stop and we refused, so he had to shoot." Later that afternoon, a deaf-mute man is shot and killed at this same junction for reasons we never learn, his death too quotidian to merit a headline.

On the far side of the junction, a teenaged boy sits beside the road holding a tray of cigarettes. The boy supplements the cigarette business by working as a passenger. Single-occupant vehicles are not permitted through the crossing for fear the drivers are suicide bombers, so he serves as a passenger for a shekel a ride. A dangerous job, and one of few opportunities in Gaza's new intifada economy. On the side we came from, another teenaged boy sits slumped beside the road, waiting to earn his shekel in the opposite direction.

We reach the refugee camp at Khan Younis, a dirty, squalid place of narrow streets and cinderblock tenements with corrugated tin roofs. The walls of the camp are covered with murals depicting soldiers, weapons, martyrs: the tableaux of everyday life. It is Friday, the Muslim holy day, so only the food market is open. Donkeys compete with cars in the street. Drivers use the horn or flash their lights but rarely employ the brake. Cars, carts and people dance a complex ballet.

We park on the western edge of the camp near a couple of Palestinian soldiers bearing Kalashnikovs. We have reached the far side of the Gush Katif settlement block. In the distance, past the concertina wire, is a collection of red-tiled roofs—a quaint, manicured village that looks as if it was air-lifted out of New Mexico. Serene as it appears, it is an odd thing to realize that a war zone exists because of it.

Around us are piles of rubble from demolished houses. A few canvas UN tents, in which no one is living, are set on top of what were once the homes facing the settlement. The buildings behind them are riddled with bullet holes and missing great chunks of mortar. Refugee kids, many of them barefoot, use the rubble, one of the few exposed places, as their playground, and clamber around inside the ruined buildings. In the rubble, I spot a piece of clothing and a small child's lone shoe.

People walk in groups along the dirt road that leads down to the Palestinian homes located next to the settlement. Above them looms a portable guard tower that has been craned onto a pole. Those who live next to the settlement cannot bring their vehicles—the chance of a bomb—and must carry special pass cards and be searched at a checkpoint before entering the area of their homes. Resident farmers transporting their produce to the market in Khan Younis must pull up their trucks, unload the produce, and then move it onto another truck to bring it out.

A voice barks orders over an army loudspeaker, barely audible from where I stand. A shot rings out, but it isn't near enough to cause me, or the crowds of refugee kids who have begun to congregate, alarm.

Through Talal, I ask the kids, mostly boys of primary school age, if they hear the fighting.

"Yes," says Mohammad, who is nine. "We hear it at night and we get very scared. Especially when I am in bed—I wake up and want to pee myself."

I ask another of the many Mohammads why he thinks the soldiers shoot.

"They want to destroy the buildings," he says. "They want to see what we are doing and they don't want us to be near them."

"One night," says an earnest, moon-faced boy in a burgundy rugby shirt, "the shooting started and my little sister, she was really scared, she started crying. When they are shooting they want us to leave our houses, but where can we go? That night we tried to escape. My parents took us outside to protect us, but when they got out they saw they forgot my sister." There are six children in his family, he says. "Sometimes from the shooting I am so afraid I cannot feel my legs."

"Do the soldiers ever talk to you?"

A chorus of assent. A small face: "Yes, they ask us how many soldiers we have over here, and who has guns."

The boys say the soldiers take shots at them while they are playing soccer. "This is the most dangerous point," one says, indicating the nearby rubble beside the fence. "They snipe."

"I advise you," says a barefoot boy in a purple-and-white-striped shirt, "if you hear any bullets, run away!"

"They killed a donkey—he's a martyr," jokes another. The kids laugh.

Do they think there will be peace one day?

"No!" All in unison.

"How can there be peace when they are killing us?" says the boy in the burgundy rugby shirt. "They are taking all of our land."

Striped purple shirt: "Even Jerusalem!"

"I like Sheik Hassan Nasrallah [secretary general of the Hezbollah in Lebanon]—he got our land back," says another, referring to Israel's forced withdrawal from Lebanon after eighteen years of military occupation. Though these children have almost certainly never left Gaza, their collective history courses through their veins.

A child of five or six leans his head against my elbow and reaches out with a tentative finger to touch the pale skin on my wrist, while an older boy steps forward to tell his story: "I was playing soccer. There, near the wire. The Israelis came to us—I saw everyone running. Suddenly I saw the jeep. Soldiers came out and put me in the jeep. They blindfolded me. They were screaming at me. They said, 'Why are you playing near the wire? Are you throwing stones?'"

It seems futile to ask it, given the place where they've grown up, but I ask anyway: do they have dreams for the future?

The boy in the burgundy rugby shirt, the one whose parents forgot his little sister, who can't feel his legs, speaks up. "I hope to become a doctor or a lawyer and to get the occupation out. To have a nice house and live with my parents in peace. And to get my land back. Not by fighting—by science and education."

In this refugee camp, a stronghold of Islamic Jihad and Hamas, where murals of fighters and mortars decorate the walls, where did he get such an idea? Did he read it, hear it from someone he admires?

"Do you think they are making any of this up?" I ask Talal as we walk back to his car, trailed by the children. Men and boys are kneeling to pray in the street because the nearby mosque is too small to hold them. A cleric's voice rings out over a loudspeaker.

"It's all true," says Talal. "If they make it up, they will make it from reality."

On the drive back, Talal reminisces about life before the closures, about going to Tel Aviv for the evening. "We could drive back at one, two in the morning, and we didn't need permission from anybody!"

He says it in the way a prisoner might speak of a fond but distant memory, like a home-cooked meal. It makes me feel ashamed of my passport, which allows me to walk effortlessly in and out of the lives of those who live here.

THE WAVES ON THE SHORES of Gaza sound the same as those in Tel Aviv. This takes me by surprise. Somehow, I had assumed they would sound different.

At Beach Camp, 75,000 refugees live in an area of less than one square kilometre in cinderblock houses with leaky roofs. Their only décor is their children.

Everywhere, tiny feet are running. Older sisters clutch the little ones, younger by just a few years. Laundry hangs from the windows; goats and chickens saunter among the children. On top of a mound of dirt, a group of kids has pounded two stakes into the ground and strung a fishnet between them. They use a soccer ball to manufacture a round of volleyball.

The men are sitting outside their homes, watching, talking, smoking. Before the closures, most of them worked as labourers in Israel. They awoke at dawn to be at the border by five. They came home in the evenings wanting only to sleep before the new workday began. Saturday, their day off, was the only day for love. Now, there is time: time to eat and sleep, time to make love to their wives. And, just as happens under curfew, more and more children will be born.

Israelis have a deep fear of the demographic onslaught. Many admit it was the inspiration for encouraging the mass immigration of Russians from the former Soviet Union, a million in the past decade; many of them, it is well known, were not Jewish. A more effective strategy in the demographic war might be this—Play It Safe: Put a Palestinian to Work.

At Beach Camp, the United Nations Relief and Works Agency provides Palestinian refugees with shelter, health care and education. UNRWA is part of the reason Palestinians are one of the best-educated populations in the Middle East. That, and the societal value accorded to education. In Saudi Arabia, Palestinian doctors are considered the very best. Money from Japan, Britain and Italy has helped to pave some of the main roads and install a sewage system at Beach Camp. In 1971, Israeli troops under Ariel Sharon's command demolished 2,000 shelters to widen the narrow roads so their jeeps could patrol them. About 8,000 refugees were moved out of the camp into a housing project in Gaza City.

Two small boys walk by, carrying a pair of ducks by their wings. Maybe for dinner, maybe as partners in play. One of the murals that cover the walls is a portrait of a boy about their size, armed with a slingshot. He is taking aim at the soldier who faces him, cocking his M-16. It is clear, even in the murals, that the artists know who is more likely to win.

Along the beach and to the right of the camp is a towering hotel, half-built, the crane frozen in motion like a fossilized idea. Tourism to Gaza? How optimistic; how painfully foolish. Hundreds of millions were invested in the mid-1990s in a dream built on shifting sands. In those days, it was not inconceivable for Israelis to contemplate travelling to Gaza as they did to Palestinian villages in the West Bank. Peace seemed near. Anything seemed possible.

A young couple, the woman wearing a hijab, sit on the shore with a small child, watching the waves time out their lives. As everywhere, there is jealousy and competition between neighbours—keeping up with the Abu Ramadans. Some think to build a new house with a cement roof to keep the rain out. Some of the homes have metal doors, others only blankets draped over the openings.

Amira Hass, a reporter for the liberal Israeli daily *Ha'aretz,* lived in Gaza for three years in the mid-1990s, before moving to the West Bank city of Ramallah. Hass, who like Roy is the child of Holocaust survivors, is currently the only Israeli journalist living among Palestinians. In her book *Drinking the Sea at Gaza,* she writes of the difficulties of daily life. One anecdote captures Palestinian frustrations and suggests that complaints may be easier to alleviate than previously thought.

"My next-door neighbor has a fantasy of kidnapping an Israeli soldier," says Abu Jamil from Jabalia. "'What will you demand in exchange?' we ask him. 'The release of all Palestinian prisoners?' 'The prisoners can go to hell,' he says. 'So what do you want?' we ask. 'More leverage for Arafat in the negotiations?' 'To hell with the negotiations,' he says. 'I just want my work permit back.' "

I AM GREETED LIKE A Western movie star at Ahmed Shawky Islamic girls' school in Gaza City. The girls, aged fourteen to sixteen, crowd around, asking me to autograph their notebooks. They are curious: I am wearing pants, travelling alone, have blonde hair, blue eyes. "We see this seldom," says the delicate Reham, the principal's daughter, who is showing me around.

Without my knowledge, a button has come undone on the bottom of my shirt. One of the girls reaches out to touch the bare skin on my stomach. She laughs. A bare midriff is taboo here. In times of poverty and conflict, adherence to Islamic custom grows stricter; even many non-religious women now wear the hijab. Here, three-quarters of the students cover their hair, though the denim skirts of their school uniform are often as tight as any Western teenager's designer jeans.

A laughing, chubby-faced girl is wearing a ring on her wedding finger. I ask her if she is married. No, she says, then runs to ask her teacher the English word. "Engaged." Her parents have arranged for her to marry her cousin as soon as she turns sixteen. Have they kissed? A flurry of laughter, covering her face with her hands: "Yes!"

"She is not very clever in school," confides Reham. "When she marries she will live in one small room with all her family, ten or fifteen people. She will cook and clean for them. In one year, two years, she will be very sad." Reham, at seventeen, is an engineering student at the Islamic University in Gaza. She hopes for a better life. Many of these girls have lost family members in the fighting. The daily sounds of Apache helicopter gunships and F-16s flying overhead can send them into hysterics.

At an office in Gaza City, I meet with Dr. Mariam Abu Daka, a former guerrilla fighter who trained in Lebanon as a teenager and is now a leader in the political arm of the Popular Front for the Liberation of Palestine, a militant organization responsible for several spectacular hijackings in the 1970s. Dr. Abu Daka has a Ph.D. in philosophy. She wears slacks and no hijab. Her dark hair is cropped short.

"Whatever we face in these black days, we will continue until we have an independent state," she says. "Even if we can't achieve it now, we won't give this suffering to the next generation."

As a funeral procession passes outside the building where we sit drinking tea, she lights a cigarette. Education is a better weapon for these girls than her years of military training, she believes. She supports three students (and nine families) on her salary. She has never married. "I am married to Palestine," she says, with a throaty laugh. "I haven't divorced it yet." But she also believes that Palestinian women have at least as much reason as men to fight the occupation.

I SIT IN ON AN AFTERNOON business meeting in a quiet office in Gaza City, listening to the rapid swish of American hundred-dollar bills being counted by practiced thumbs. Deals are cash-only, conducted between Gazan businessmen whose families preceded the refugees and still control most of the wealth. An elastic band snaps around a thick wad of dollars that is left on the table in view. One man, sporting a short black beard, a well-cut suit and a gold watch set with diamonds, says he lost a million dollars this year. When peace seemed near he made good money. Now, all the construction has stopped. The land he bought for US$600,000 is worth half that today. He could not sell it if he wanted to. The half-million he invested in Saudi Arabia grew by half again in the same time span, but he doesn't want to invest his money outside of Gaza. This is where he lives. This is where his family lives. This is where he wants their future to be.

So he should buy low, I suggest. Sure, he shrugs. He is buying. But what about selling high? Who says values will rise? Only the donkey sellers are making money. The price of a donkey has risen ten times since cars were forbidden on certain roads and gasoline grew scarce.

"So who's the donkey? Who's the donkey? Tell me—who's the donkey now?"

CHAPTER 11

The Making of a Martyr

Wall murals, Gaza City

"THERE ARE THREE things in the world that are powerful," Talal Abu Rahma tells me, pulling sagely on his moustache. "Money, women and journalism."

He sees in me, I suspect, a younger journalist keen to absorb his insights. For if news is the main commodity of the Gaza Strip, Talal is one of its chief exporters. He knows how to slip a tape from his news camera and drop it into his waistband, exchanging it for a blank that he dutifully hands over when the soldiers demand it. He has been arrested six times by Israeli security forces and three times by the Palestinian Authority. In his office is a picture of him at a demonstration for press freedom in front of the Palestinian parliament building in Gaza City. He is smiling broadly and carrying a sign that reads, in English: "NO FOR SHUTTING UP OUR MOUTHS."

I meet Talal at his office and we take a drive along the main coastal road, past the place where Mohammad al-Durrah was killed. It happened on September 30, 2000, two days into the second intifada. Mohammad was the first child to die in this war, and his death was witnessed around the world. I recall standing in my living room in Canada, preoccupied with something else, when my gaze snapped to his death unfolding on my television screen.

The junction is called Netzarim by Israelis, because it fronts on the Jewish settlement of Netzarim, and Martyr's Junction by Palestinians, because it is where so many Palestinians have died. Any Palestinian travelling from the southern Gaza refugee camps to Gaza City must pass by the junction, where boys and young men gather to throw stones at the symbols of occupation.

Today, tanks are positioned on the barren swath of land, facing traffic. There is no trace of the cement barrel Mohammad al-Durrah and his father took refuge behind, nor of the Palestinian security shack that once stood there. These and a pair of nearby apartment buildings were razed by the Israeli army shortly after the boy's death—to deny Palestinian gunmen cover, the army said. We drive past slowly. Talal has turned off the music, opened the windows.

From inside the tanks, pairs of eyes peer out. Though it is hard to be sure from a distance, the eyes seem fearful. This despite, or perhaps because of, the massive artillery advantage and the sheltering bodies of the tanks. Once, when Israeli journalist Amira Hass was travelling in the occupied territories, a soldier asked her if she was afraid. After all, he had a gun and he was afraid; she was unarmed. Perhaps, Hass speculated, it was his weapon that gave him reason to fear.

Talal was in the area the day al-Durrah died, filming clashes between Israeli soldiers and Palestinian security forces. He had taken shelter behind a van when he noticed the father and son huddled opposite the

Israeli military post. He heard the boy cry out and trained his camera on the pair. While he was filming, Charles Enderlin reached him by cell phone and lectured him for leaving his flak jacket and helmet in his car. Talal, still under fire, switched off the phone and continued to film.

An ambulance driver died trying to rescue the boy and his father; a Palestinian police officer died trying to rescue the boy, the father and the ambulance driver. But it was the boy, dying in his father's arms, whose image Talal captured.

In the footage, the boy is shielded by his father. The father is crouched down, shouting and waving for the soldiers to stop firing. The boy cries out as bullets strike his body. One hits him in the abdomen, and he bleeds to death in his father's arms before help can arrive.

"Nearly as soon as French television cameraman Talal Abu Rahma captured the scenes, young Mohammad's visage become synonymous with the unfathomable aggression, and the resulting global rage," wrote the *Middle East Times*. "His face has been stenciled on walls throughout the occupied territories, and his death replayed time and time again over martial music that has no doubt fanned pan-Arab outrage."

Arab leaders rode the wave. Jordan Television showed King Abdullah at the boy's father's bedside in Amman, where Jamal al-Durrah spent four months recovering in hospital. Muammar Qadhafi appeared with al-Durrah on Libya's Jamahiriya Television, and saluted him with his trademark raised fist.

The "Palestinian pietà," the image was called in one of the innumerable reports, commentaries and op-eds churned out in the following days, weeks and months. Mohammad al-Durrah became a symbol of opposition to Israeli occupation. A martyr among martyrs.

For the past year Talal has been travelling to international journalism festivals to collect awards. I ask him about the ways his life has been affected. Fame, for instance, carries certain risks in his line of work. Forty-five journalists were injured by bullets in the occupied territories in the year since Mohammad al-Durrah's death—three-quarters of them

Palestinian, according to Reporters Without Borders, and most of the shots fired by Israeli forces. So for a time Talal heeded warnings, dyeing his white hair black before going to the front lines. Now he has let the white return. He says he won't dye his hair again.

In Gaza, he says, vendors believe the footage has made him a million-aire, so they try to charge him inflated prices. They don't understand that he works on salary and doesn't earn royalties. In the Arab world, he has been criticized for refusing to use his position as a platform to criticize Israel. But more than these nuisances, he is irritated by charges that he used his profession to further the Palestinian cause.

"I think these people, they don't need me to defend them, you know," he says. He repeats his mantra: "Journalism is my religion, jour-nalism is my nationality, journalism is my language."

"Do you ever wonder what the family's life would be like if you had not taken the footage?" I ask him. "Do you ever regret that Mohammad's parents never have a day free from it?"

"But the father was there," Talal says, his voice rising. "It's not only the picture that reminds the family of Mohammad. No, no, no. How about the father? He saw it, he felt it, they shot on him. The picture shocked the world. And showed the truth of what is happening."

In the past, Talal and the al-Durrah family have refused all media requests to be interviewed together. This day, Talal decides to pay the al-Durrahs a visit. The questions I've asked have pricked him. Bring your recording equipment, he says.

THE BUREIJ REFUGEE CAMP IS typical—poorly built cement homes, hordes of children playing in the narrow sandy streets—except that on almost every wall is spray-painted the face of Mohammad al-Durrah.

A jolt. Someone rear-ends the car.

"Son of a camel!" growls Talal.

He gets out, but the damage is too minimal to bother with, and what does it matter when no one can afford to pay? We park and children clamber around the car while Talal makes a mild effort to keep them from climbing on it. One of the children, a little brother to Mohammad, is the boy's spitting image. Since Mohammad's death, the al-Durrah family home has become a shrine to his memory. On the outside wall of the house is a fresco of the father and son in the boy's final moments.

Talal knocks at the door. The father answers—the familiar gaunt face. Jamal al-Durrah is surprised and backs away, almost closing the door in Talal's face. It takes a moment for him to recover from his shock at seeing the man who is so intimately intertwined with the strange course his life has taken, and to gain the composure to invite us inside.

Otherwise, the al-Durrahs have grown accustomed to media attention. Plucked out of obscurity for the tragic renown reserved for the parents of a dead hero, Jamal and his wife, Amal, have spent the past year in a whirlwind of media interviews, public appearances and travel. They who had left Gaza only once before have now been to Algeria, Egypt, the United Arab Emirates and the international conference on racism in Durban, South Africa.

Mohammad is described by most as an active child, the second-oldest, fun-loving, family favourite. That morning, his father had suggested they go to a used-car market in Gaza City. He thought it would be a good idea to keep his inquisitive son away from the flashpoints. Ariel Sharon had just completed his controversial visit to the Temple Mount/Haram ash-Sharif area in East Jerusalem flanked by a thousand Israeli police and soldiers, an act that was viewed as an assertion of Israeli dominance over the location of two of the oldest Muslim shrines. Riots were breaking out. Sentiments were tinder-hot.

Jamal and Mohammad never found a car. They took a taxi home from the market but were stalled at Netzarim while Palestinian policemen stopped traffic to allow ambulances to pass through. Father and son left the taxi and cut across a nut field, a route they thought was away from the clashes. It was there that they became the targets of sustained gunfire.

For the al-Durrahs, their son's death takes place every day. They cannot enter or leave their home without reminders, in the murals, in the relentless recycling of the footage on Arab and Palestinian TV, in the lyrics of songs written by popular Arab musicians. Amal al-Durrah, quiet and pretty, brings out small cups of sweet mint tea. She says her six surviving children—who shriek and run wildly around the house while the parents seem oblivious—sing the pop songs about Mohammad. It took her weeks to be able to look at the footage, but she says she has grown accustomed to it. Now, when it appears on TV, she feels Mohammad is still with her somehow.

Today the image of father and son is emblazoned on souvenir T-shirts for sale in Gaza City, alongside images of that other revolutionary icon, Che Guevara, and the kitsch inflatable Yasser Arafats so popular with visiting CIA agents. It appears in a promo for Al Jazeera, beamed into the homes of thirty-five million Arab viewers for whom Mohammad al-Durrah has become a household name. It shows up, as well, on the Arabic toilet paper roll covers that Jamal al-Durrah came across one day, which distressed him greatly, he says, "because this is a symbol and a martyrdom. The next day people take the roll cover and throw it in the garbage." Jamal says he was also angered by the Jewish group in New York who edited the image, placing kipas on his head and Mohammad's to make them look Jewish, the targets of Palestinian bullets.

Then there are the rumours of the family's sudden wealth. The al-Durrahs received the standard compensation for Palestinian families of victims: a monthly pension worth US$40 from the Palestinian Authority, and a lump sum of US$10,000 from Saddam Hussein, whose face peers down from a poster on their wall. Funds for the family were collected throughout the Islamic world, but Jamal al-Durrah says none of the money reached him or any Palestinian. Their box-like home is furnished with white plastic chairs and a child's bed as a sofa—a Barbie doll among their children's toys is the only sign of affluence—but a social worker told Jamal he no longer qualifies for aid because, apparently, King Abdullah of Jordan has given him a palace.

Jamal is angered by these accusations. "Of course I would leave my home and live in the palace," he says sarcastically. "I wouldn't live in the house that fills up with water in the winter."

Like the parents of fallen soldiers, the al-Durrahs want to believe their son's death was not in vain. For a time, it appeared that might actually be the case. "Can the image of one little boy dying change the world?" asked a newspaper headline. The footage shocked the international community, refuting Israel's claim that its soldiers don't target civilians. Commentators speculated that the child's death might lead to a turning point and inspire Western intervention. That didn't happen.

"I want to see the film," Jamal is saying to Talal. Three weeks earlier, Talal showed the footage at the local cultural centre.

"But you were there," Talal says. Jamal had been in the audience.

"I couldn't look at it," says Jamal.

"You didn't see it?"

"No. I didn't look at it. I didn't have the guts to look at it."

Talal asks him if there are times he wishes the footage hadn't been taken.

"No," says Jamal. "Even if I didn't see these pictures on the TV, or anywhere else, his picture is always in my mind because Mohammad was beside me when he got killed. The pain is already there inside me because my son was on my lap. I was defending him."

He says he will never forgive the Israelis, for whom he used to work as a house painter. "But I am sorry to say that nobody condemned this. And there are a lot of crimes the Israeli soldiers committed against our people and nobody filmed them. This is terrible." He falls silent. "Stop, I cannot continue."

THE AL-DURRAH INCIDENT WAS A major embarrassment for the Israeli army. In Israeli media, coverage focussed mainly on the follow-up investigation. The general commanding the area, General Yom-Tov Samia, told CBS correspondent Bob Simon that he would clear the name of the Israeli soldiers involved. Since the actual location had been destroyed, the army staged a re-enactment that aired on *60 Minutes*.

The show drew sharp criticism from some Israelis, including a Labor parliament member who labelled the re-enactment "fictitious." CBS later quoted reports that the investigators commissioned by General Samia had not been actual ballistic experts, and noted that at least one of the investigators had stated publicly, prior to the investigation, that he was convinced Palestinians had shot the boy.

As part of their investigation, which they later deemed inconclusive, the army asked France 2 for a tape of the footage. Charles Enderlin, a consummate newsman with a voice like sandpaper, has been covering the Middle East for three decades. He provided them with a copy of the tape but refused to participate in the investigation, because to him it resembled "a whitewash."

"They said they found, on our video, traces of bullets coming from behind. We didn't find such traces on the video," he says.

The investigation also questioned what father and son were doing in a war zone. Enderlin repeats what I already know: the area is a major crossroad for residents of Gaza. Enderlin asked for permission to interview the soldiers involved and to send a camera crew to film the angles of shooting against the ones documented in the army's final report, but his requests were denied.

"This is something very strange which I couldn't understand," he says. "I heard that they came later on with interviews of soldiers, but what are they worth after six months, after one year?"

Later, the Israeli army chief of staff told Israel's parliament that General Samia had acted alone, and that the army was investigating his actions.

From the outset, Enderlin decided to waive the usual agency fees and give away the footage. "From a simple ethical point of view, I don't believe that we could have made money off the death of Mohammad al-Durrah," he says. "Or any other child, by the way. If it would have been a Jewish child being killed in front of the camera, I believe our reaction would have been the same."

Enderlin, who is Jewish, has faced his own share of fallout for airing the story. "I got the Israeli extreme right on my back; there were death threats. We also got the extreme right of the Jewish French-speaking community here. My wife and my two young kids were also threatened. We had to put private guards at night around our home. This was quite unpleasant." Since then they have moved and changed their phone number.

I mention the public-relations battles the story has engendered, but Enderlin shrugs it off. "The psychology of people related to this very strong picture, that is another story for me. As journalists, Talal and I are not philosophers. We cover the news daily. We stick to the facts. And we try to show the reality of what happens here. For us, the sad story of Mohammad al-Durrah belongs to the sad reality of this region."

ON MY LAST AFTERNOON IN Gaza, Talal drives me through the northern village of Beit Hanoun. Kids are barefoot, playing in the street, moving out of the way when they hear the horn. A flock of goats has managed to get inside a trio of metal garbage containers and they are feasting contentedly, a cloud of flies orbiting their gently bobbing heads.

Talal turns down a side road and pulls up in front of a rusted gate. Three Palestinian soldiers are seated on the ground. They are sharing a water pipe between them. A fire is lit for tea.

The soldiers scramble to their feet. One retrieves his Kalashnikov from where he had set it down. They try to look professional. Across the way is an Israeli settlement. They are supposed to be keeping an eye on things, but more likely they are trying to stay out of the way. Most of the Palestinian police stations stand empty, as they are regular targets of attack.

Talal parks in front of the gate and honks the horn for a long time, but no one comes. He gets out and pounds on the gate with his fist for a long, long time. Eventually the gate opens, and we drive through.

This is the farm his family owns. The trees are heavy with oranges and lemons. At the end of a row of orange trees a group of orange pickers are filling boxes and piling them into a donkey's cart. Some of the trees are short and stubby, just beginning to bear fruit. They were planted to replace those cut down by Gazans for firewood during the first closures of the Gulf War.

The man who opened the gate, the overseer, wears loose cotton pants, his head gently swathed in a white cotton turban. He picks a handful of perfect oranges and peels them for us with his knife. They taste better than mandarin oranges, sweeter than the Israeli oranges grown in the north.

The overseer brings me more oranges to put in my daypack, for I am leaving this place. They are the sweetest oranges I have ever tasted, and I wonder if it is like water in the desert, so sweet because I am in a bitter place. But I will think the same thing later, back in Jerusalem, where the weather has turned cold and rainy, and I am peeling and eating one alone.

When Talal drives me to the border crossing, he leaves me on the Palestinian side. I make the final journey across by myself. My taxi driver is a handsome young Israeli just back from an extended trip to New York, where he made a good living selling factory-made paintings by posing as an art student and going door-to-door. Now he is a courier for the news agencies, delivering packages and transporting journalists. Lapel pins from Reuters, AP, ABC, CNN and a host of others adorn his dashboard. He offers me a cigarette and we make the usual small talk about the hopeless situation. It is a surprisingly short ride to Jerusalem—in traffic, under an hour. As we ascend the hill to the city, we stop at a light. A group of ultra-Orthodox wearing black suit jackets and white dress shirts cross in front of the taxi. "I hate the penguins," the driver says.

We pass the bus station, where someone has spray-painted a greeting: "Shalom Messiah."

"Welcome to civilization," he says.

Epilogue

Arab market on David Street, Jerusalem

I AM WAITING IN ZION Square on Jerusalem's Ben Yehuda Street. A dread-locked musician sits on the stony ground playing the didgeridoo, its mournful strains trailing through the outdoor pedestrian mall. Behind him, a soldier sits on a bench, scribbling in a notebook. I glance into the window of a souvenir store at a sun-faded T-shirt that reads "Guns 'n' Moses" and another, with a Nike swoosh, that reads "Torah—Just Do It." The sky overhead threatens rain, and the heavy garments of the ultra-Orthodox are beginning to look practical. I keep watch for the grey toque Rotem Mor has told me he will be wearing.

Two young men have congregated, talking, at the far end of Zion

Square, both wearing light-grey toques. I approach them and introduce myself. The taller, lankier one is Mor; the other, in wire-rimmed glasses, is Noam Kuzar, who just happened to be walking by. Both are twenty years old, and both are among the growing number of Israeli "refuse-niks": army conscripts, soldiers and reserve soldiers who, for reasons of conscience, refuse to fulfill their military service.

Mor suggests we all have coffee at a place he knows. Down a narrow alley and up a flight of stairs, we find a table in a dimly lit, book-lined café, a bohemian backpacker hangout.

Mor tells me he was a soldier-teacher in the Israel Defense Forces. Slowly, doubts about his service began to plague him. "I didn't want to enslave myself to something I didn't believe in," he says. A year and a half into his three years of mandatory service, he removed his uniform and asked to be released. A military committee refused to review his case when he showed up at the hearing in civilian clothing. In the end, he was sentenced to twenty-eight days in prison.

Mor calls himself a pacifist—he rejects, in general, the military solution. In a statement he published before his arrest, he wrote: "For a long time, I have had doubts about the honesty of military service. These questions began to arise long before I was drafted. They stemmed from information I had acquired about the Israeli-Arab conflict, and from discovering the false information about it, to which I was exposed for years. As I learned more, I was increasingly skeptical about the official Israeli version of what happened. This official version is the basis on which most of Israeli youth justifies its military service. I started to understand to what extent fear and hatred had been instilled in me from a very early age. I discovered that I do not believe in the existence of an 'enemy,' but rather in the existence of people of different cultures, who are frightened and angry, just like me."

Noam Kuzar is not a pacifist, but rather a "selective refuser": he accepts certain justifications for the use of force, such as the defence of borders, but rejects others, such as the suppression of Palestinian revolt.

"The IDF is a necessary tool, but as a tool it depends how you use it," he says. He paraphrases psychologist Abraham Maslow, a pioneer in the understanding of human motivations: "If the only tool you have is a hammer, every problem begins to look like a nail."

On October 2, 2000, Kuzar's combat unit was given four hours' notice that they were being reassigned to the West Bank to guard a settlement. "I said, I'm not going, not passing the Green Line"—shorthand for Israel's pre-1967 borders—"not going one metre past the border," he tells me. Kuzar had informed his superiors from the time he enlisted that he was willing to defend Israel's borders, but "the territories aren't Israel," and he wasn't willing to fight for them. "There are three million Palestinians there who don't have the right to vote, who can't have a regular job or go to school without soldiers standing over them," he says. When faced with the order, he became the first soldier of this intifada to refuse to go to the occupied territories. He served two twenty-eight-day prison terms for his stance.

I ask Mor and Kuzar if they have any Arab or Palestinian friends. Neither of them does.

"There aren't many places for Jews and Arabs to meet," explains Kuzar.

"It's the nature of war," adds Mor. "If we were mixed together it would be much harder to fight one another. It would be much harder to go up on a roof and shoot at them. Like I can't go onto Noam's roof and shoot his sister. If I knew 'Mohammad,' I couldn't prevent him from going to work."

According to New Profile, an Israeli anti-militant organization that supports conscientious objectors such as Kuzar and Mor, the number of Israeli refuseniks has grown dramatically since the eruption of violence in September 2000. Partly it's because people are more aware of human rights violations in the occupied territories; partly it's because Israeli youth, exposed to global pop culture, are questioning the allegiances with which they were raised. Many others do not openly refuse, but take the traditional route of visiting a psychiatrist and pleading emotional problems.

A milestone for the refusenik movement came in an open letter dated September 3, 2001, from sixty-two Israeli teenagers to Prime Minister Ariel Sharon. Its contents shocked the country, generating angry debate.

"We strongly resist Israel's pounding of human rights," the letter reads. "Land expropriation, arrests, executions without a trial, house demolition, closure, torture, and the prevention of health care are only some of the crimes the state of Israel carries out, in blunt violation of international conventions it has ratified.

"These actions are not only illegitimate; they do not even achieve their stated goal—increasing the citizens' personal safety. Such safety will be achieved only through a just peace agreement between the Israeli government and the Palestinian people.

"Therefore we will obey our conscience and refuse to take part in acts of oppression against the Palestinian people, acts that should properly be called terrorist actions. We call upon persons our age, conscripts, soldiers in the standing army, and reserve service soldiers to do the same."

Seventeen-year-old Haggai Matar, one of the letter's organizers, told the *Guardian* newspaper, "The way I see it, the army is one big conquering army. It is not the Israeli Defense Forces. It is a conquering army that does more wrong, more harm than good."

But most Jewish Israelis, with the exception of the ultra-Orthodox, who are exempted from service, still view military service as a hallowed rite of passage. The IDF is considered above reproach—above, even, political considerations—and perspectives such as these are seen as a kind of heresy. Even many left-wing groups have proven unwilling to publicly endorse the refuseniks. "You are still the minority," I tell Kuzar and Mor.

"For now," Kuzar says. "I think more and more people see that the situation in the occupied territories is not right. Most soldiers are drafted right after high school. I think the future refuseniks will come from the reserves, people who have had time to live a little."

SINCE MY DEPARTURE FROM THE Middle East at the end of November 2001, the situation in Israel and the occupied territories has threatened to spiral out of control. Despite its virtual re-occupation of the entire West Bank and its siege of Palestinian leader Yasser Arafat at his compound in Ramallah, Israel has been unable to prevent suicide bombers from striking at the heart of its civilian population. The "Gaza-ization" of the West Bank is well underway—IDF raids have left not only a trail of bodies and razed houses but a devastated civil infrastructure, including, according to the United Nations High Commissioner for Human Rights, destruction of Palestinian Authority ministries (such as the Ministry of Industry, the Ministry of Education, the Ministry of Civilian Affairs and the Land Registration Office), and damage to medical facilities, schools, municipalities, religious buildings, and the buildings of relief and development organizations. The development of a Palestinian civil society—the best mechanism for tempering violence—has been set back by years, if not decades. Perhaps the most chilling development was a relatively minor one, quickly reversed when it came to light: the writing of numbers on the arms of some Palestinian detainees.

In February 2002, two hundred Israeli reserve soldiers, among them high-ranking combat officers, lived up to Noam Kuzar's prediction and ignited a firestorm of controversy in Israel and the rest of the world by signing the now-famous Combatants' Letter: "We hereby declare that we shall continue serving in the Israel Defense Forces in any mission that serves Israel's defense," they wrote. "The missions of occupation and oppression do not serve this purpose—and we shall take no part in them."

If there are any glints of light in this dark time, it is these brave few, those who preceded them and those who have joined them since. If anything breaks the back of the occupation, it will be those who refuse to stand by, who add their voices to the rising chorus—within Israel and the international community—demanding justice and an end to the vicious game.

May the promise of a homeland be fulfilled for all of Abraham's children, Arab and Jew.

ACKNOWLEDGEMENTS

THIS BOOK COULD NEVER HAVE been written without the input of people too numerous to mention who shared their stories and their dinner tables, offered words of advice and caution, revealed where to buy the best hummus and pita, and tolerated my questions with good humour and insight.

I am particularly grateful for the generous assistance provided by Candace, David, Doron, Leat, Maged, Reuven, Shula, Talal, Yoel and, above all, Ken, without whom this book might never have been written. A special thanks goes to Lynne Bowen, Cynthia Hopkins and Barbara Pulling for their editorial counsel. My mention of these persons in no way implies that they endorse the contents of the book; any errors are, of course, my own.

CHRONOLOGY

1516–1917   Palestine becomes part of Ottoman Empire.

1878   First modern Jewish settlement established in Petach Tikva.

1882–1903   First Aliyah (wave of Jewish immigration) arrives in Palestine, mainly flee-
            ing persecution in Russia and Romania.

1891   Arab notables in Jerusalem petition Ottoman government to prohibit Jewish
            immigration and land purchases.

1896   Austrian journalist Theodor Herzl, founder of modern political Zionism,
            publishes *The Jewish State*, which advocates establishing a Jewish state in
            Palestine or elsewhere to end persecution.

1897   Herzl convenes first Zionist Congress in Basel, Switzerland, which calls for the
            establishment of a Jewish "home in Palestine" and "the colonization of
            Palestine by Jewish agricultural and industrial workers."

1904–14   Second Aliyah from Eastern Europe.

1909   Founding of first kibbutz, Degania, and first modern Jewish city, Tel Aviv.

1915–16   Correspondence between Sharif Husayn of Mecca and Sir Henry McMahon,
            British High Commissioner in Egypt, assures Arabs of postwar independence
            and unity of Arab provinces (including Palestine) of Ottoman Empire.

1916   Sykes-Picot Agreement carves up moribund Ottoman Empire between Britain
            and France. Britain wins control over Palestine.

1917   British Foreign Secretary Arthur J. Balfour issues Balfour Declaration, pledg-
            ing British support for a "national home for the Jewish people" in Palestine,
            with the understanding that "nothing shall be done which may prejudice the

civil and religious rights of existing non-Jewish communities."

1919	First Palestinian National Congress in Jerusalem rejects Balfour Declaration and demands independence.
1919–23	Third Aliyah, mainly from Russia.
1920	Palestine Mandate assigned to Britain. Founding of Haganah, a Jewish underground military organization.
1921	Anti-Zionist riots in Jaffa.
1922	Churchill White Paper states that tensions in Palestine are due to Arab "apprehensions" "partly based upon exaggerated interpretation" of Balfour Declaration. First British census finds Palestine population 78 per cent Muslim, 11 per cent Jewish, 10 per cent Christian.
1924–32	Fourth Aliyah, mainly from Poland.
1929	Arab riots in Jerusalem. British troops reinstate order.
1933–39	Fifth Aliyah, mainly from Germany.
1936–39	Arab revolt uses violence to protest establishment of a Jewish national home.
1937	Britain's Peel Commission recommends partitioning Palestine.
1937–39	Irgun, a Jewish militant organization, plants bombs in Arab buses and marketplaces.
1939	British White Paper restricts Jewish immigration and land acquisition.
1944–47	Jewish militant groups target British rule, assassinating Lord Moyne in Cairo and bombing Jerusalem's King David Hotel.
1947	United Nations votes to partition Palestine into a Jewish state and a Palestinian Arab state, with Jerusalem as an international enclave. Jewish leaders object to internationalizing Jerusalem but accept proposal; Arabs reject it.
1948	Britain leaves Palestine. Israel declares independence. Egypt, Jordan, Lebanon, Syria and Iraq join with Palestinians to fight establishment of a Jewish state. Jordan occupies West Bank and East Jerusalem, Egypt the Gaza Strip. More than 200 Palestinians killed by Jewish militants at Deir Yassin. Some 700,000 Palestinian refugees flee or are forced from their homes. UN mediator Count Folke Bernadotte assassinated by a Jewish militant group to thwart his efforts to modify partition plan.
1949	Armistice agreements between Israel and Egypt, Jordan, Lebanon and Syria, but not Iraq.
1950	Israel's parliament passes Law of Return, granting every Jew right to citizenship in Israel. Large-scale immigration ensues, mainly from Europe and Arab countries.
1951	Israel ratifies Fourth Geneva Convention on Rules of War, established in

	1949 to prevent a recurrence of Nazi atrocities in occupied Europe.
1956	Israel joins Britain and France in Sinai Campaign, attacking Egypt under Gamal Abdel Nasser and occupying most of Sinai Peninsula. Pressure from U.S. and USSR persuades Israel to withdraw.
1964	Nasser leads Arab heads of state in establishing Palestine Liberation Organization (PLO) in Cairo.
1967	Israel launches preemptive attacks on Egypt, Syria and Jordan in Six-Day War, which ends with Israel occupying East Jerusalem, West Bank, Gaza Strip, Sinai Peninsula and Golan Heights. Second exodus of Palestinian refugees. UN Security Council Resolution 242 establishes "land for peace" formula, calling for withdrawal of Israeli armed forces from "territories occupied" and "just settlement" for refugees.
1968	Establishment of Jewish settlement in Hebron. PLO hijacks El Al airliner.
1969	Yasser Arafat becomes PLO chairman.
1970–71	Battle between Jordan and PLO ends with PLO expulsion to Lebanon. Egypt seeks peace treaty with Israel under the Labor government of Golda Meir, who turns down the offer.
1972	Eleven Israeli athletes killed at Munich Olympics by a Palestinian group calling itself Black September.
1973	Yom Kippur War. Egypt and Syria attack Israeli forces in Sinai Peninsula and Golan Heights but are driven back. UN Security Council Resolution 338 calls for implementation of Resolution 242.
1974	Arab Summit in Rabat recognizes PLO as sole legitimate representative of Palestinian people. UN General Assembly reaffirms Palestinian right to national independence and PLO gains UN "observer status." Yasser Arafat addresses General Assembly calling for a united Palestine for Muslims, Christians and Jews under a democratic secular government.
1977	Egyptian President Anwar Sadat addresses Israeli parliament in Jerusalem. Settlement activity accelerates under Likud government.
1979	Egypt and Israel sign peace agreement.
1982	Israel withdraws from Sinai. Under Defense Minister Ariel Sharon, Israel invades Lebanon with stated aim of eliminating PLO, leading to 17,500 mainly civilian deaths. PLO evacuates Beirut and establishes headquarters in Tunisia. Israel's Phalangist allies kill 1,500 in Palestinian refugee camps of Sabra and Shatilla while Israeli forces surround the camps.
1985	Israel bombs PLO headquarters in Tunisia.

1987–90	First *intifada* or "shaking off," a popular Palestinian uprising against Israeli rule in occupied territories.
1988	Palestinian National Council recognizes Israel's right to exist, proclaims a Palestinian state and calls for negotiations. U.S. begins diplomatic talks with PLO.
1991	Gulf War. Iraq launches missiles at Israel; Palestinian support for Iraq has dire consequences. Peace conference convened in Madrid. Large-scale aliyah from former Soviet republics continues for the next decade.
1992	Yitzhak Rabin elected Israeli prime minister.
1993	Israel and PLO agree in Oslo to mutual recognition and limited self-rule for Palestinians, sealed by a handshake between Rabin and Arafat. Arafat and PLO return to Gaza, promising to renounce violence.
1994	Jewish settlement growth accelerates. Israeli troops clash with Palestinians protesting construction of Efrat settlement. A Jewish settler shoots worshippers at a Hebron mosque. Jordan and Israel sign peace treaty. First Palestinian suicide bombing in Afula.
1995	Israeli Prime Minister Yitzhak Rabin assassinated.
1996	First Palestinian elections. Yasser Arafat is voted president of Palestinian Authority. In Jerusalem, Hamas claims responsibility for a bus bombing that kills nineteen.
1997	Israel commits to settlement expansion in Jordan Valley.
1998	U.S.-brokered Israel-Palestinian Wye Memorandum signed to "facilitate" implementation of previous agreements on security arrangements and Israeli withdrawal from sections of occupied territories.
2000	Israel withdraws from southern Lebanon. Talks deadlock between Yasser Arafat and Israeli Prime Minister Ehud Barak at Camp David. Israeli opposition leader Ariel Sharon visits Temple Mount/Haram ash-Sharif area in Jerusalem. Palestinian riots turn into "Al-Aksa intifada." Barak resigns.
2001	Barak suspends negotiations in Taba. Ariel Sharon defeats Barak to become Israel's prime minister.

SOURCES

BOOKS

Bellow, Saul. *To Jerusalem and Back: A Personal Account.* New York: Viking Press, 1976.

Elon, Amos. *Jerusalem, City of Mirrors.* Boston: Little, Brown & Company, 1989.

Friedman, Robert I. *Zealots for Zion: Inside Israel's West Bank Settlement Movement.* New York: Random House, 1992.

Gavron, Daniel. *The Kibbutz: Awakening from Utopia.* New York: Rowman & Littlefield, 2000.

Gellhorn, Martha. *The Face of War.* New York: Simon & Schuster, 1959.

Hass, Amira. *Drinking the Sea at Gaza: Days and Nights in a Land under Siege.* New York: Henry Holt and Company, 1996.

Hodgkins, Allison B. *Israeli Settlement Policy in Jerusalem: Facts on the Ground.* Jerusalem: PASSIA, December 1998.

Leviatan, Uriel, Hugh Oliver and Jack Quarter, eds. *Crisis in the Israeli Kibbutz: Meeting the Challenge of Changing Times.* Westport, CT: Praeger Publishers, 1998.

Richler, Mordecai. *This Year in Jerusalem.* New York: Alfred A. Knopf, 1994.

Roy, Sara. *The Gaza Strip: The Political Economy of De-Development.* Washington, DC: Institute for Palestine Studies, 1995.

Said, Edward. *Peace and Its Discontents: Essays on Palestine in the Middle East Peace Process.* New York: Vintage Books, 1996.

Simpson, John. *A Mad World, My Masters.* London: Macmillan, 2000.

REPORTS

The Democracy and Workers' Rights Center in Palestine. "Annual Report 2000," February 2001.

Remez, Didi. "15 New Settlement Sites since the Elections," May 20, 2001. <www.peacenow.org.il/>

"Report of the High Commissioner for Human Rights submitted pursuant to decision 2002/103," April 24, 2002. <http://domino.un.org/unispal.nsf>

Reporters Without Borders. "Case Study of 45 Journalists Injured by Bullets in the Occupied Territories from September 2000," August 2001. <www.rsf.org>

United Nations. "Geneva Convention Relative to the Protection of Civilian Persons in Time of War." <www.hri.ca/uninfo>

UNSCO. "Impact on the Palestinian Economy of Confrontation, Border Closures and Mobility Restrictions: 1 October 2000 to 30 June 2001."

UNSCO. "Impact on the Palestinian Economy of Confrontation, Border Closures and Mobility Restrictions: 1 October 2000 to 30 September 2001." <http://domino.un.org/unispal.nsf>

WEB SITES

<http://domino.un.org/unispal.nsf> UNISPAL—United Nations Information System on the Question of Palestine

<www.arts.mcgill.ca/mepp/prrn/prfront.html> Palestinian Refugee ResearchNet

<www2.iol.co.il/btselem> B'Tselem, the Israeli Information Center for Human Rights in the Occupied Territories

<www.coalitionofwomen4peace.org> Coalition of Women for Peace

<www.couragetorefuse.org> Web portal for international supporters of Israeli refusers

<www.medea.be> European Institute for Research on Mediterranean and Euro-Arab Cooperation

<www.mfa.gov.il> Israel Ministry of Foreign Affairs

<www.un.org/unrwa> The United Nations Relief and Works Agency

NEWSPAPER AND MAGAZINE ARTICLES

Ackerman, Seth. "Losing Ground." *Harper's Magazine,* December 2001.

Associated Press. "Israeli Settlements Plan Growth." May 26, 2001. <www.peacenow.org.il>

Barzilai, Amnon. "More Israeli Jews Favor Transfer of Palestinians, Israeli Arabs—Poll Finds." March 13, 2002. <www.haaretzdaily.com>

Bassok, Moti, and Reuters. "Israeli Population Growth in Territories Drops Sharply." December 19, 2001. <www.haaretzdaily.com>

Bond, Michael. "This Is How We Live." *New Scientist,* May 11, 2002.

Boucek, Christopher. "Satellites Beam Uprising across the Region." *Middle East Times,* October 13, 2000. <www.metimes.com>

Dayan, Aryeh. "Tunnel Vision." *Ha'aretz,* October 8, 2001.

Goldenberg, Suzanne. "The Right Not to Fight." *Guardian of London,* September 7, 2001.

Goldenberg, Suzanne. "Israel Defies US with Settlement Expansion Plans." *Guardian of London,* May 30, 2001. <www.guardian.co.uk>

Ha'aretz Service. "Poll: Arabs Miss Rabin More Than Jews Do." *Ha'aretz,* November 6, 2001.

Harel, Amos. "NIS 250 M Allocated for New Gaza Fences." January 17, 2002. <www.haaretzdaily.com>

Ilan, Shahar. "Haredim May Get Gender-Separated Bus Line." *Ha'aretz,* October 24, 2001.

Levine, Joni. "Center for Jewish Living Hosts Chief Rabbi from Israel." *Cornell Daily Sun,* April 24, 2001.

Marcus, Jonathan. "Secularism vs Orthodox Judaism." BBC News, April 22, 1998. <http://news6.thdo.bbc.co.uk>

"Probing Root Causes of Mideast Violence." CBS News, November 12, 2000. <www.cbsnews.com>

Riskin, Shlomo. "Mass Expression of Pain." *The Jerusalem Post,* August 20, 1995.

"The Settlement Burden on the Budget." December 27, 2001. <www.haaretzdaily.com>

Shragai, Nadav. "Jews Buy up Land around Jerusalem Simon Hatzadik Neighborhood." *Ha'aretz,* October 12, 2001.

INTERVIEWS

Abu Daka, Mariam. Interviewed in Gaza City, November 2001.

Abu Rahma, Talal. Interviewed in Gaza City, November 2001.

Al-Durrah, Jamal and Amal. Interviewed at Bureij refugee camp, Gaza, November 2001.

Bitterman, Dita. Interviewed in Tel Aviv, September 2001.

Eid, Bassem. Interviewed in Jerusalem, November 2001.

Enderlin, Charles. Interviewed in Jerusalem, November 2001.

Espanioly, Nabila. Interviewed in Nazareth, September 2001.

Kuzar, Noam. Interviewed in Jerusalem, November 2001.

Matar, Nadia. Interviewed in Jerusalem, November 2001.

Mor, Rotem. Interviewed in Jerusalem, November 2001.

Rollins, Greg. Interviewed in Hebron, September 2001.

Riskin, Rabbi Shlomo. Interviewed in Jerusalem, October 2001.

Schlesinger, Mike. Interviewed at Kibbutz Ma'agan Mikhael, October 2001.

Weber, George. Interviewed in Hebron, September 2001.